SMALL
CROSS STITCH
PATTERNS

**90+ Mini Counted Designs
with Birds, Animals, Plants, Food,
Various Objects, and More**

(up to 40x40 Crosses)

CONTENTS

CONTENTS

CONTENTS

CONTENTS

CONTENTS

CONTENTS

HOW TO READ A CROSS STITCH CHART

A cross stitch chart shows you the colors and location of every stitch. One colored square (with a symbol) on a chart corresponds to a single stitched square on your fabric. A thread legend shows a list of all embroidery colors, and which symbol belongs to which DMC floss number.

Thin lines separate stitches from each other, and thick lines separate every ten stitches for easy counting.

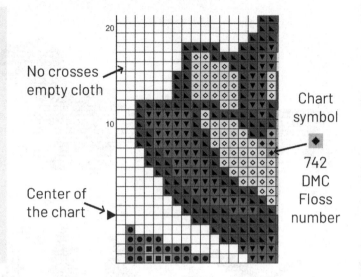

No crosses empty cloth

Chart symbol

742 DMC Floss number

Center of the chart

FABRIC

Each project in this book uses **Aida 14** cloth. It is the most common cotton evenweave fabric with small holes for easier counting and needle insertion. The number 14 means that you can sew 14 crosses on a length of 1 inch.

If you prefer to stitch smaller versions, you can use Aida 16 or 18. If you want to stitch bigger designs, you can use Aida 11.

FLOSS

Each project uses **DMC floss** (six-stranded cotton floss). It is the most widely used brand of embroidery thread. Each color has its own number, which is shown in a thread legend.

Use 2 strands of thread for Aida 14 cloth embroidery.

NEEDLE

A cross stitch needle has a blunt tip (less chance of pricking your fingers) and a bigger eye. Cross stitch needles have different sizes (**needle size 24 for Aida 14**, needle size 26 for Aida 16, needle size 28 for Aida 18 cloth and needle size 22 for Aida 11 cloth).

■ **Hoop** (wood, bamboo, plastic). You can stitch with or without hoop. Aida cloth has enough stiffness to allow you to stitch without hoop. Try both options and decide which is more convenient for you. The most common is the 6" hoop size, it feels more comfortable in your hands when stitching.

■ **Scissors** for cutting thread or cloth.

■ Water-soluble fabric **marker** and **pencil**.

■ **Measuring tape** or a ruler.

■ **Anti-fraying liquid** for sealing the edges of your fabric (just an extra handy option).

LET'S START CROSS STITCHING

Place the needle tip into the bottom left corner from the back of the cloth **(1)** and stitch the front of the cloth toward the top right corner **(2)**. Then place the needle tip into the right bottom corner from back of the cloth **(3)** and stitch the front of the cloth toward to the top left corner **(4)**. You now have a cross stitch!

If you have more than one cross in a row of the same thread color, you can stitch the whole row at once. First make right slanted stitches, and then left slanted stitches that cover them.

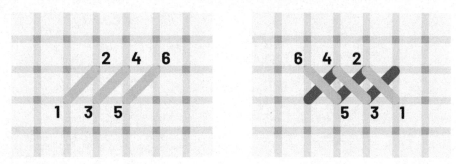

You can stitch right slanted or left slanted stitches first: it makes no difference. Just make sure you have **one direction** for the whole work.

TIPS

Always wash your hands before you start embroidery.

Try to find time to double-check stitch quantity. It helps to avoid mistakes.

Add 3-4 extra inches for each side before cutting the cloth. It will help neatly frame your work after finishing.

Start cross stitching from the center of the fabric. Fold the fabric in half with your finger along the fold, then fold it in half again. Straighten it out and you will see the center — mark it with a water-soluble fabric marker.

After you have finished your embroidery, hand-wash it gently with a soft detergent and iron on the back side between two towels.
Allow the fabric to dry naturally and frame it if necessary.

For each project, you will need up to 6 DMC colors

Up to 40x40 crosses for each project

Only full cross stitches

Let's begin!

DESIGN 01

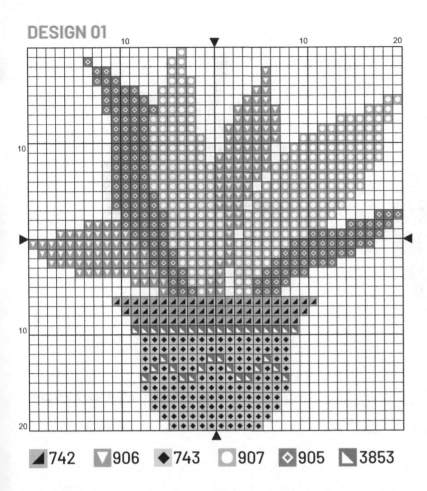

Fabric: 14 count White Aida
Colors: DMC
Stitches: 40 x 40
Size: 2.86 x 2.86 in / 7.26 x 7.26 cm

Use 2 strands of thread for cross stitch

◣ 742   ▽ 906   ◆ 743   ◯ 907   ◇ 905   ◹ 3853

DESIGN 02

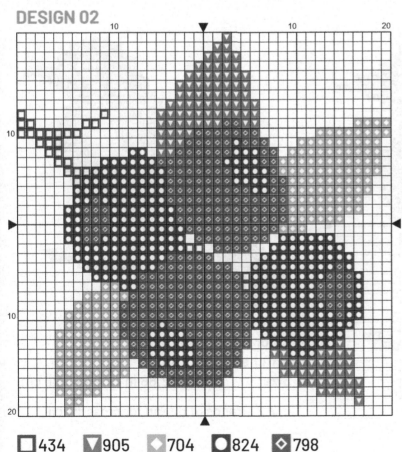

Fabric: 14 count White Aida
Colors: DMC
Stitches: 40 x 40
Size: 2.86 x 2.86 in / 7.26 x 7.26 cm

Use 2 strands of thread for cross stitch

▢ 434   ▽ 905   ◇ 704   ◯ 824   ◈ 798

13

DESIGN 03

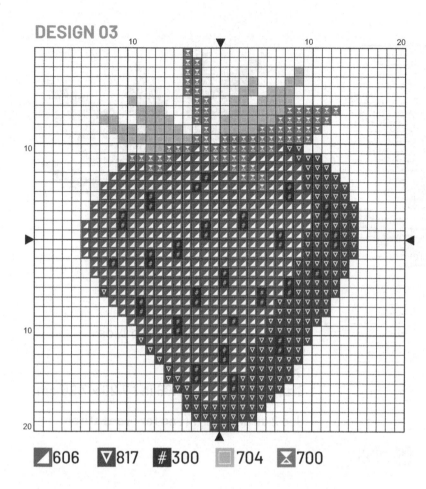

Fabric: 14 count White Aida
Colors: DMC
Stitches: 30 x 40
Size: 2.14 x 2.86 in / 5.44 x 7.26 cm

Use 2 strands of thread for cross stitch

◢606 ▽817 #300 ☐704 ⊠700

DESIGN 04

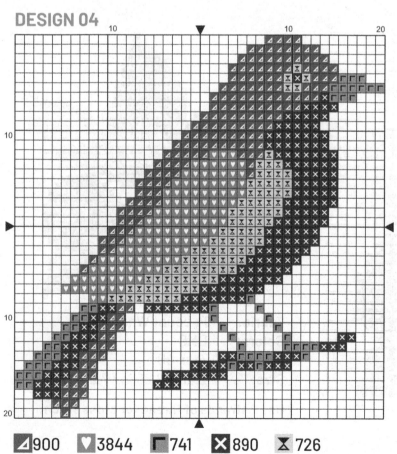

Fabric: 14 count White Aida
Colors: DMC
Stitches: 40 x 40
Size: 2.86 x 2.86 in / 7.26 x 7.26 cm

Use 2 strands of thread for cross stitch

◢900 ♥3844 ⌐741 ✕890 ⊠726

DESIGN 05

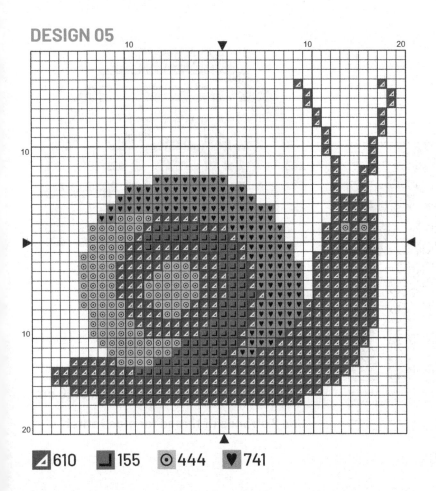

Fabric: 14 count White Aida
Colors: DMC
Stitches: 37 x 34
Size: 2.64 x 2.43 in / 6.71 x 6.17 cm

Use 2 strands of thread for cross stitch

◢ 610   ⌐ 155   ⊙ 444   ♥ 741

DESIGN 06

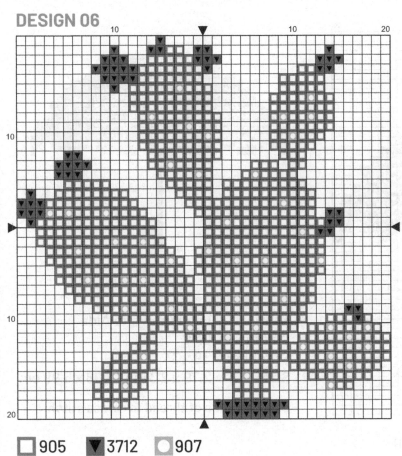

Fabric: 14 count White Aida
Colors: DMC
Stitches: 40 x 40
Size: 2.86 x 2.86 in / 7.26 x 7.26 cm

Use 2 strands of thread for cross stitch

☐ 905   ▼ 3712   ◯ 907

DESIGN 07

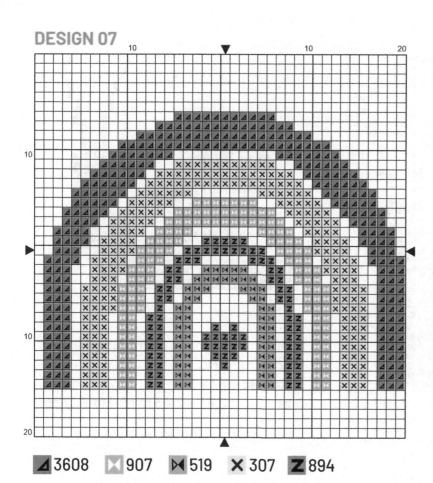

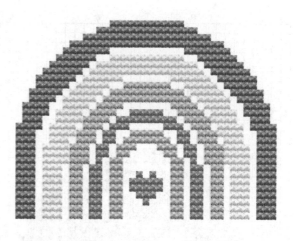

Fabric: 14 count White Aida
Colors: DMC
Stitches: 39 x 29
Size: 2.79 x 2.07 in / 7.08 x 5.26 cm

Use 2 strands of thread for cross stitch

◢ 3608 ◨ 907 ◧ 519 ✕ 307 ▨ 894

DESIGN 08

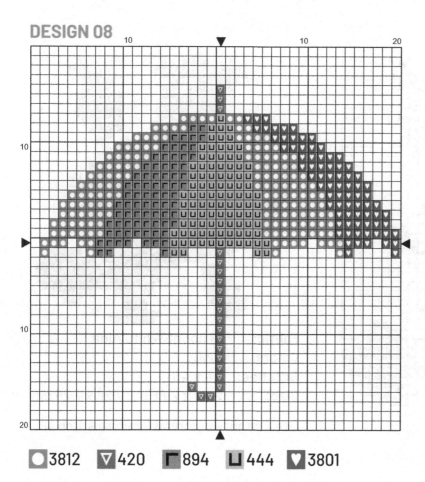

Fabric: 14 count White Aida
Colors: DMC
Stitches: 39 x 33
Size: 2.79 x 2.36 in / 7.08 x 5.99 cm

Use 2 strands of thread for cross stitch

◯ 3812 ▽ 420 ⌐ 894 ⊔ 444 ♡ 3801

16

DESIGN 09

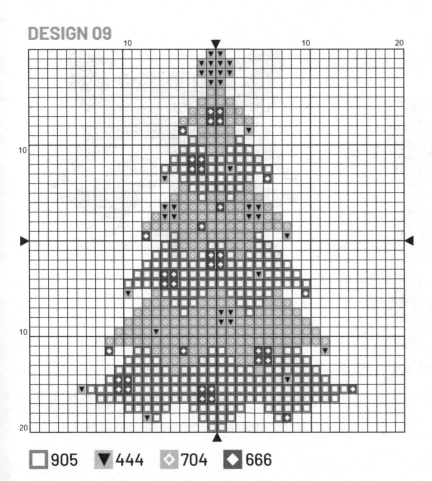

Fabric: 14 count White Aida
Colors: DMC
Stitches: 30 x 40
Size: 2.14 x 2.86 in / 5.44 x 7.26 cm

Use 2 strands of thread for cross stitch

☐ 905 ▼ 444 ◇ 704 ◆ 666

DESIGN 10

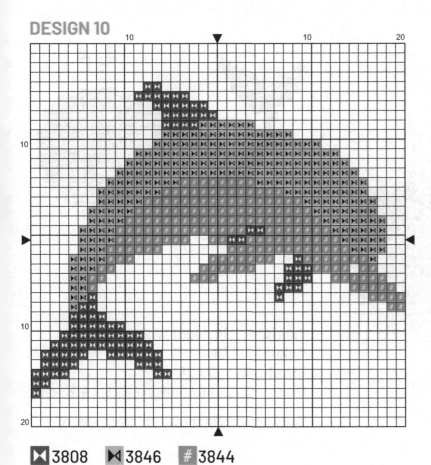

Fabric: 14 count White Aida
Colors: DMC
Stitches: 40 x 33
Size: 2.86 x 2.36 in / 7.26 x 5.99 cm

Use 2 strands of thread for cross stitch

⋈ 3808 ⋈ 3846 # 3844

DESIGN 11

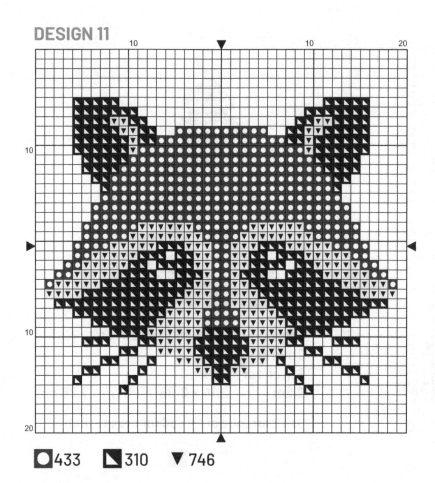

Fabric: 14 count White Aida
Colors: DMC
Stitches: 38 x 31
Size: 2.71 x 2.21 in / 6.89 x 5.62 cm

Use 2 strands of thread for cross stitch

⊙ 433   ◤ 310   ▼ 746

DESIGN 12

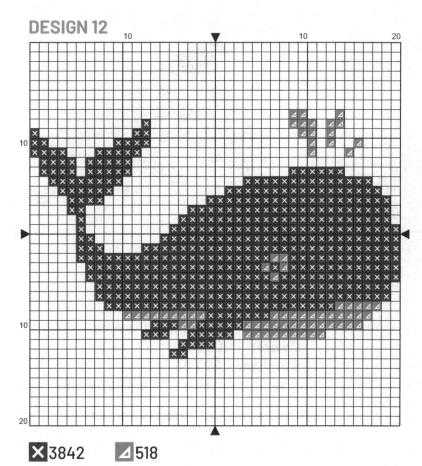

Fabric: 14 count White Aida
Colors: DMC
Stitches: 40 x 26
Size: 2.86 x 1.86 in / 7.26 x 4.72 cm

Use 2 strands of thread for cross stitch

✖ 3842   ◹ 518

DESIGN 13

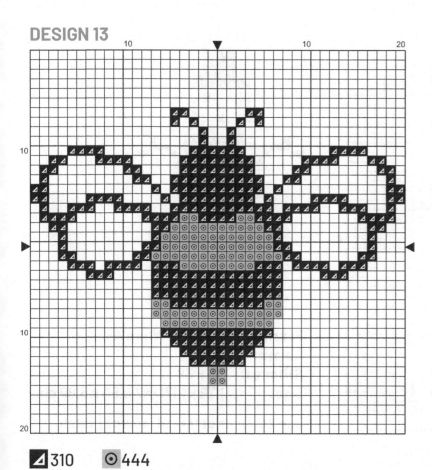

Fabric: 14 count White Aida
Colors: DMC
Stitches: 40 x 29
Size: 2.86 x 2.07 in / 7.26 x 5.26 cm

Use 2 strands of thread for cross stitch

◪ 310   ⊙ 444

DESIGN 14

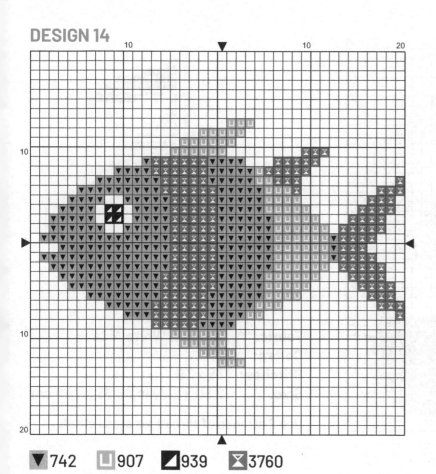

Fabric: 14 count White Aida
Colors: DMC
Stitches: 39 x 26
Size: 2.79 x 1.86 in / 7.08 x 4.72 cm

Use 2 strands of thread for cross stitch

▼ 742   ⊔ 907   ◪ 939   ⊠ 3760

DESIGN 15

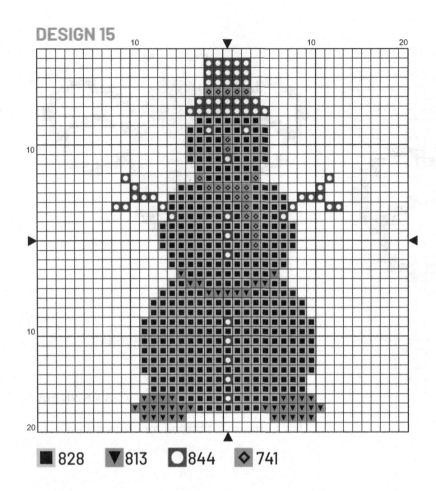

Fabric: 14 count White Aida
Colors: DMC
Stitches: 25 x 38
Size: 1.79 x 2.71 in / 4.54 x 6.89 cm

Use 2 strands of thread for cross stitch

■ 828   ▼ 813   ◎ 844   ◇ 741

DESIGN 16

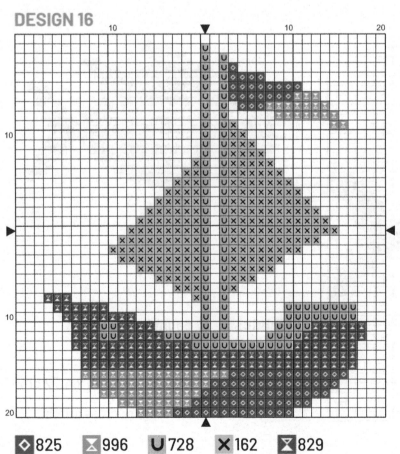

Fabric: 14 count White Aida
Colors: DMC
Stitches: 35 x 39
Size: 2.50 x 2.79 in / 6.35 x 7.08 cm

Use 2 strands of thread for cross stitch

◇ 825   ⊠ 996   U 728   ✕ 162   ⊠ 829

DESIGN 17

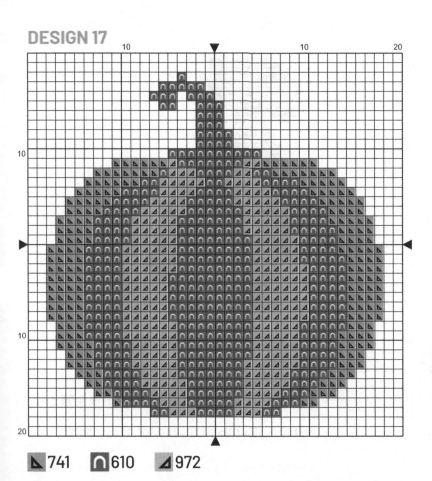

Fabric: 14 count White Aida
Colors: DMC
Stitches: 36 x 36
Size: 2.57 x 2.57 in / 6.53 x 6.53 cm

Use 2 strands of thread for cross stitch

◥ 741   ◠ 610   ◿ 972

DESIGN 18

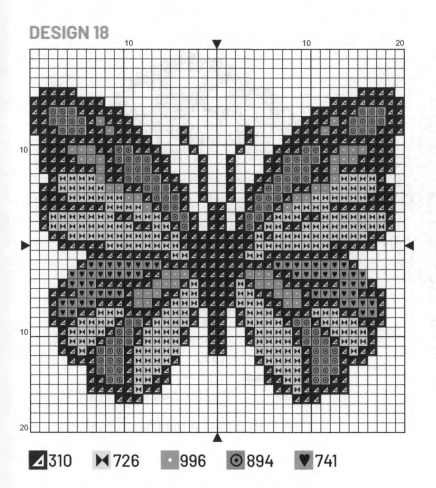

Fabric: 14 count White Aida
Colors: DMC
Stitches: 40 x 33
Size: 2.86 x 2.36 in / 7.26 x 5.99 cm

Use 2 strands of thread for cross stitch

◿ 310   ⋈ 726   · 996   ⊙ 894   ♥ 741

DESIGN 19

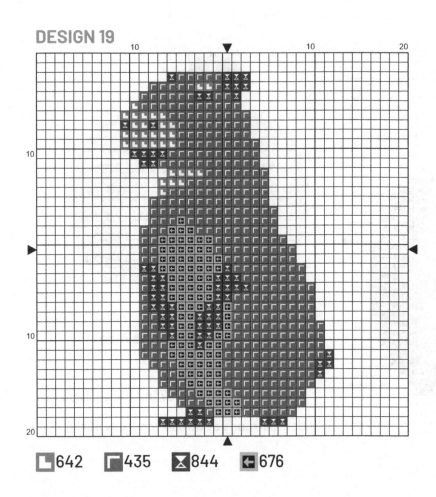

Fabric: 14 count White Aida
Colors: DMC
Stitches: 23 x 37
Size: 1.64 x 2.64 in / 4.17 x 6.71 cm

Use 2 strands of thread for cross stitch

☐ 642 ☐ 435 ☒ 844 ☐ 676

DESIGN 20

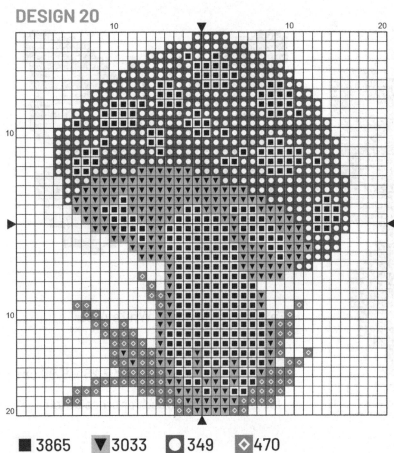

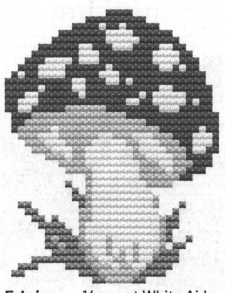

Fabric: 14 count White Aida
Colors: DMC
Stitches: 32 x 40
Size: 2.29 x 2.86 in / 5.81 x 7.26 cm

Use 2 strands of thread for cross stitch

■ 3865 ▼ 3033 ◯ 349 ◇ 470

DESIGN 21

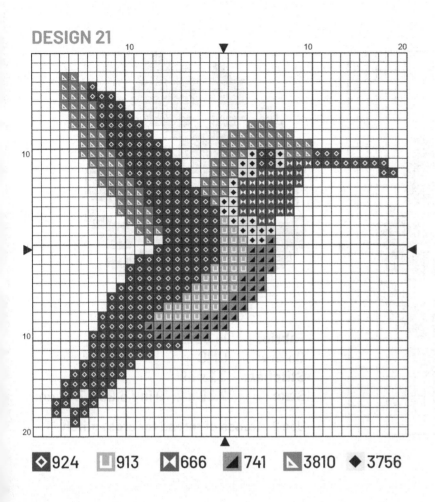

Fabric: 14 count White Aida
Colors: DMC
Stitches: 37 x 37
Size: 2.64 x 2.64 in / 6.71 x 6.71 cm

Use 2 strands of thread for cross stitch

◇ 924   ⊔ 913   ◤ 666   ◣ 741   ◹ 3810   ◆ 3756

DESIGN 22

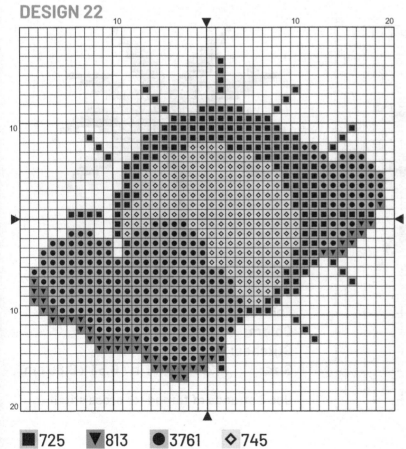

Fabric: 14 count White Aida
Colors: DMC
Stitches: 38 x 34
Size: 2.71 x 2.43 in / 6.89 x 6.17 cm

Use 2 strands of thread for cross stitch

■ 725   ▼ 813   ● 3761   ◇ 745

DESIGN 23

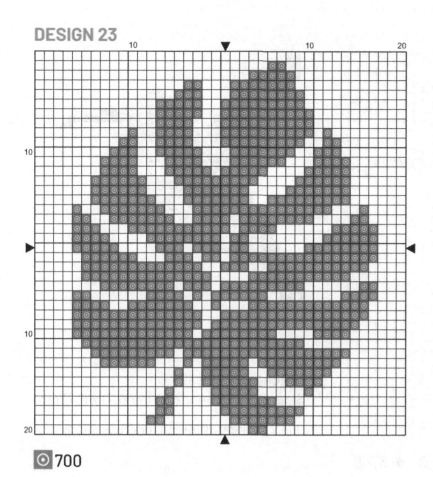

Fabric: 14 count White Aida
Colors: DMC
Stitches: 33 x 39
Size: 2.36 x 2.79 in / 5.99 x 7.08 cm

Use 2 strands of thread for cross stitch

◉ 700

DESIGN 24

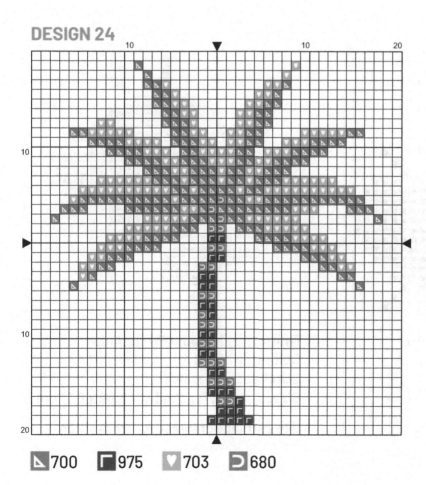

Fabric: 14 count White Aida
Colors: DMC
Stitches: 36 x 38
Size: 2.57 x 2.71 in / 6.53 x 6.89 cm

Use 2 strands of thread for cross stitch

◣ 700   ◰ 975   ♥ 703   ⊃ 680

DESIGN 25

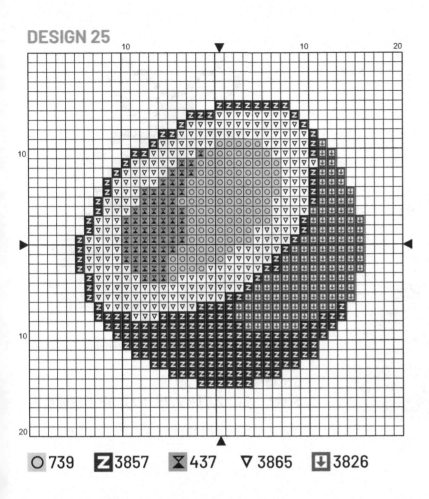

Fabric: 14 count White Aida
Colors: DMC
Stitches: 31 x 30
Size: 2.21 x 2.14 in / 5.62 x 5.44 cm

Use 2 strands of thread for cross stitch

○ 739   Z 3857   ✕ 437   ▽ 3865   ⬇ 3826

DESIGN 26

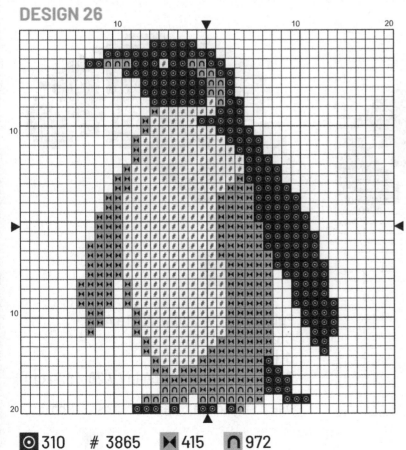

Fabric: 14 count White Aida
Colors: DMC
Stitches: 28 x 39
Size: 2.00 x 2.79 in / 5.08 x 7.08 cm

Use 2 strands of thread for cross stitch

◉ 310   # 3865   ◪ 415   ∩ 972

DESIGN 27

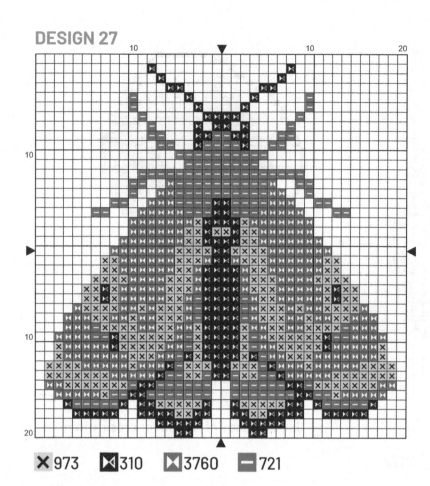

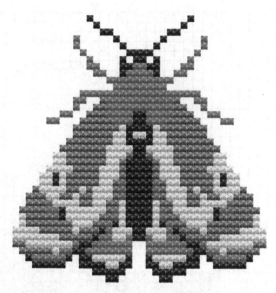

Fabric: 14 count White Aida
Colors: DMC
Stitches: 38 x 39
Size: 2.71 x 2.79 in / 6.89 x 7.08 cm

Use 2 strands of thread for cross stitch

✖ 973 ◪ 310 ◪ 3760 — 721

DESIGN 28

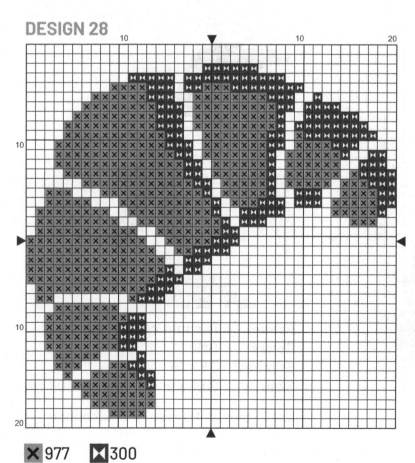

Fabric: 14 count White Aida
Colors: DMC
Stitches: 40 x 37
Size: 2.86 x 2.64 in / 7.26 x 6.71 cm

Use 2 strands of thread for cross stitch

✖ 977 ◪ 300

DESIGN 29

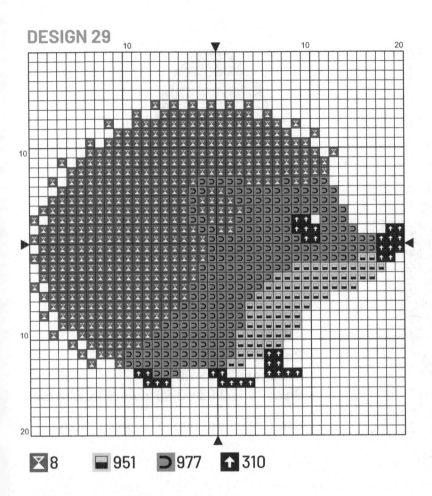

Fabric: 14 count White Aida
Colors: DMC
Stitches: 40 x 30
Size: 2.86 x 2.14 in / 7.26 x 5.44 cm

Use 2 strands of thread for cross stitch

⊠ 8   ▥ 951   ⊃ 977   ⬆ 310

DESIGN 30

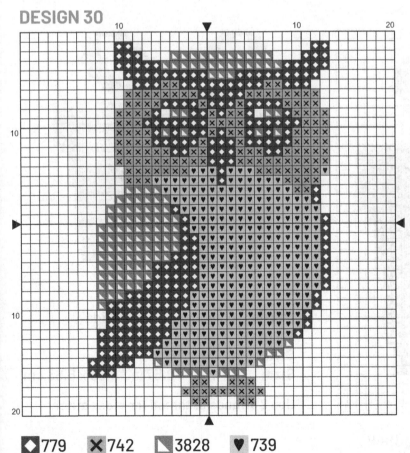

Fabric: 14 count White Aida
Colors: DMC
Stitches: 26 x 38
Size: 1.86 x 2.71 in / 4.72 x 6.89 cm

Use 2 strands of thread for cross stitch

◆ 779   ✕ 742   ◩ 3828   ♥ 739

27

DESIGN 31

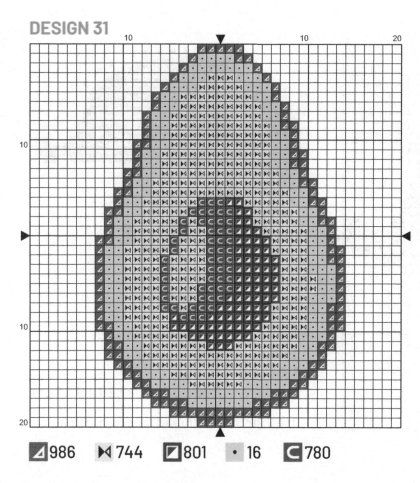

Fabric: 14 count White Aida
Colors: DMC
Stitches: 27 x 40
Size: 1.93 x 2.86 in / 4.90 x 7.26 cm

Use 2 strands of thread for cross stitch

◢ 986　◄► 744　◢ 801　• 16　C 780

DESIGN 32

Fabric: 14 count White Aida
Colors: DMC
Stitches: 36 x 36
Size: 2.57 x 2.57 in / 6.53 x 6.53 cm

Use 2 strands of thread for cross stitch

▼ 3750　◢ 3849　◻ 931　◄► 3340　▭ 3848

DESIGN 33

Fabric: 14 count White Aida
Colors: DMC
Stitches: 38 x 35
Size: 2.71 x 2.50 in / 6.89 x 6.35 cm

Use 2 strands of thread for cross stitch

◢ 725   ■ 311   ◉ 3844   ▽ 310

DESIGN 34

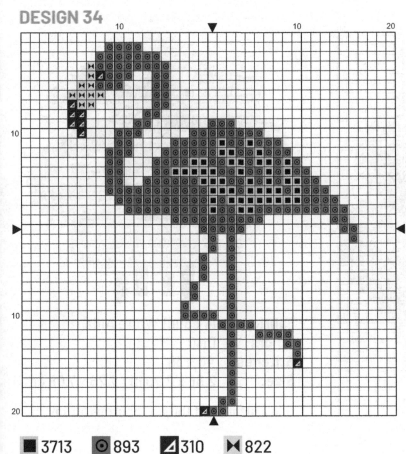

Fabric: 14 count White Aida
Colors: DMC
Stitches: 31 x 39
Size: 2.21 x 2.79 in / 5.62 x 7.08 cm

Use 2 strands of thread for cross stitch

■ 3713   ◉ 893   ◢ 310   ⋈ 822

DESIGN 35

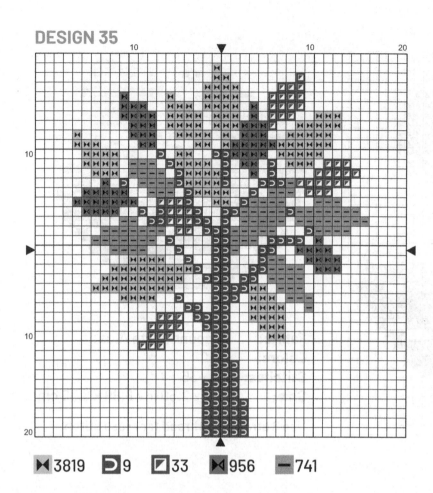

Fabric: 14 count White Aida
Colors: DMC
Stitches: 32 x 39
Size: 2.29 x 2.79 in / 5.81 x 7.08 cm

Use 2 strands of thread for cross stitch

3819 9 33 956 741

DESIGN 36

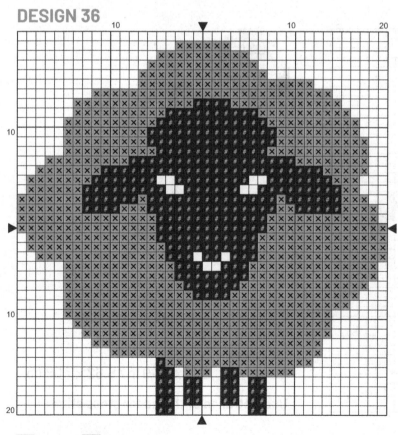

Fabric: 14 count White Aida
Colors: DMC
Stitches: 40 x 39
Size: 2.86 x 2.79 in / 7.26 x 7.08 cm

Use 2 strands of thread for cross stitch

415 310

DESIGN 37

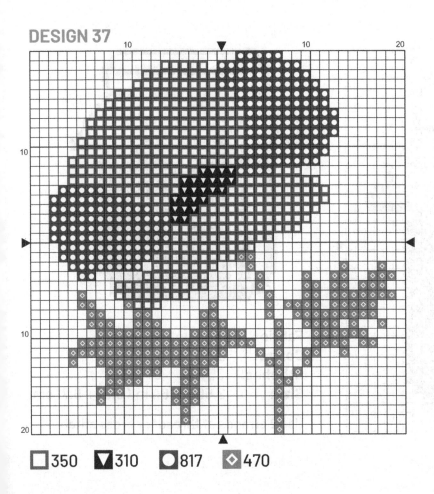

Fabric: 14 count White Aida
Colors: DMC
Stitches: 37 x 40
Size: 2.64 x 2.86 in / 6.71 x 7.26 cm

Use 2 strands of thread for cross stitch

□ 350 ▼ 310 ⬤ 817 ◇ 470

DESIGN 38

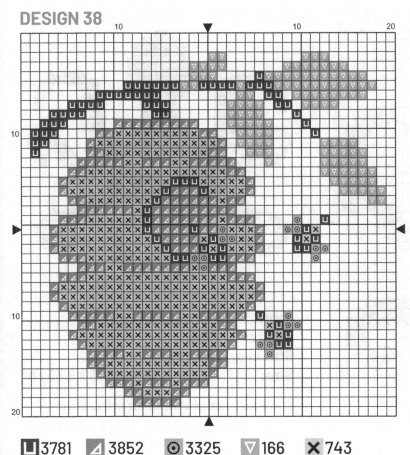

Fabric: 14 count White Aida
Colors: DMC
Stitches: 38 x 37
Size: 2.71 x 2.64 in / 6.89 x 6.71 cm

Use 2 strands of thread for cross stitch

Ц 3781 ◿ 3852 ⊙ 3325 ▽ 166 ✕ 743

DESIGN 39

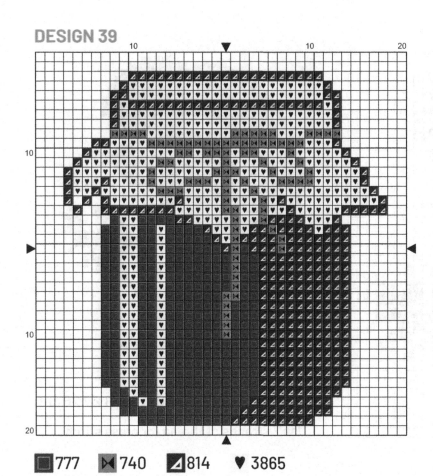

Fabric: 14 count White Aida
Colors: DMC
Stitches: 35 x 37
Size: 2.50 x 2.64 in / 6.35 x 6.71 cm

Use 2 strands of thread for cross stitch

⬜ 777   ◪ 740   ◢ 814   ♥ 3865

DESIGN 40

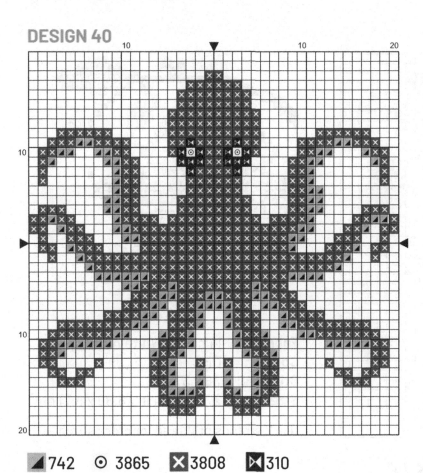

Fabric: 14 count White Aida
Colors: DMC
Stitches: 40 x 36
Size: 2.86 x 2.57 in / 7.26 x 6.53 cm

Use 2 strands of thread for cross stitch

◢ 742   ⊙ 3865   ✖ 3808   ◪ 310

DESIGN 41

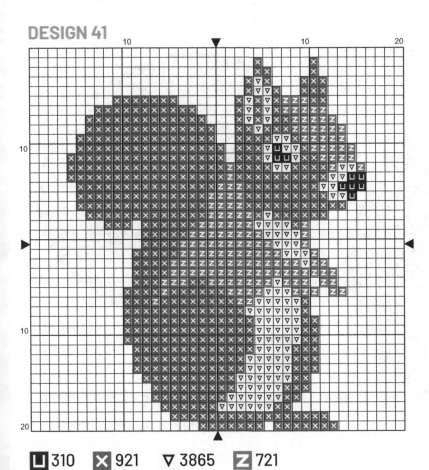

Fabric: 14 count White Aida
Colors: DMC
Stitches: 32 x 39
Size: 2.29 x 2.79 in / 5.81 x 7.08 cm

Use 2 strands of thread for cross stitch

U 310 X 921 ▽ 3865 Z 721

DESIGN 42

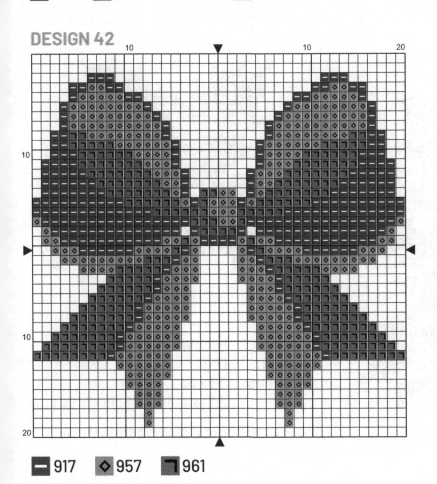

Fabric: 14 count White Aida
Colors: DMC
Stitches: 40 x 37
Size: 2.86 x 2.64 in / 7.26 x 6.71 cm

Use 2 strands of thread for cross stitch

— 917 ◇ 957 ⌐ 961

DESIGN 43

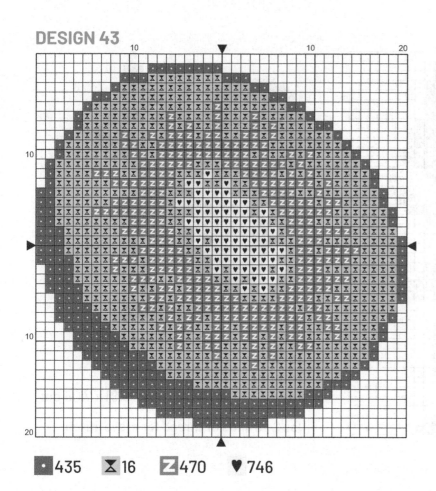

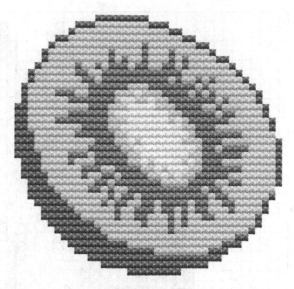

Fabric: 14 count White Aida
Colors: DMC
Stitches: 40 x 38
Size: 2.86 x 2.71 in / 7.26 x 6.89 cm

Use 2 strands of thread for cross stitch

● 435   ✕ 16   Z 470   ♥ 746

DESIGN 44

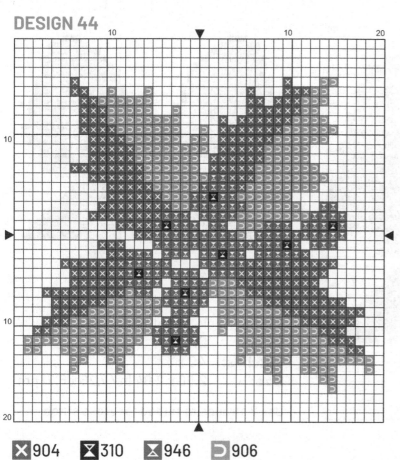

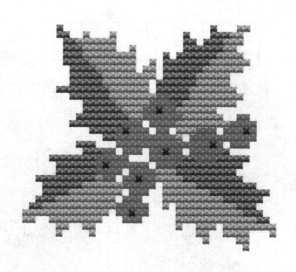

Fabric: 14 count White Aida
Colors: DMC
Stitches: 38 x 33
Size: 2.71 x 2.36 in / 6.89 x 5.99 cm

Use 2 strands of thread for cross stitch

✕ 904   ✕ 310   ✕ 946   ⊃ 906

DESIGN 45

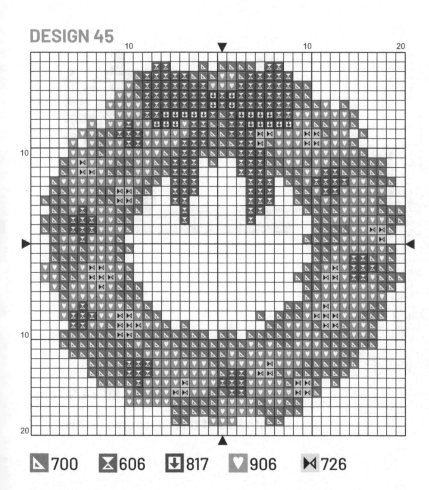

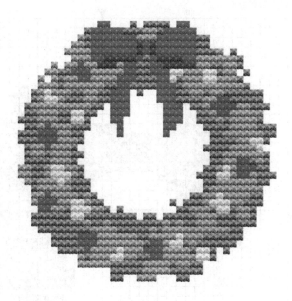

Fabric: 14 count White Aida
Colors: DMC
Stitches: 39 x 38
Size: 2.79 x 2.71 in / 7.08 x 6.89 cm

Use 2 strands of thread for cross stitch

◣ 700   ⧗ 606   ⬇ 817   ♥ 906   ⋈ 726

DESIGN 46

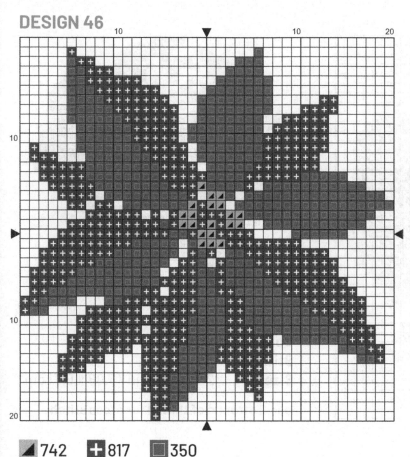

Fabric: 14 count White Aida
Colors: DMC
Stitches: 40 x 39
Size: 2.86 x 2.79 in / 7.26 x 7.08 cm

Use 2 strands of thread for cross stitch

◣ 742   ✚ 817   ◻ 350

DESIGN 47

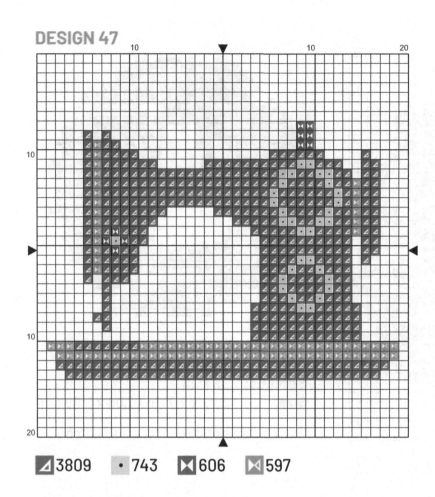

Fabric: 14 count White Aida
Colors: DMC
Stitches: 38 x 27
Size: 2.71 x 1.93 in / 6.89 x 4.90 cm

Use 2 strands of thread for cross stitch

◪ 3809 • 743 ◪ 606 ◪ 597

DESIGN 48

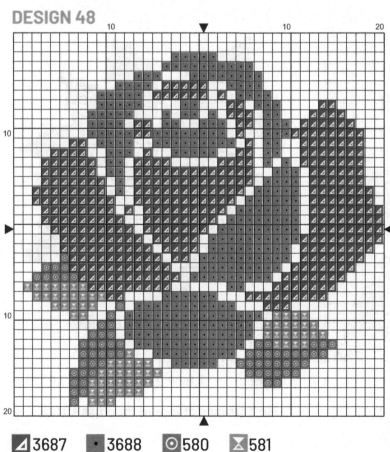

Fabric: 14 count White Aida
Colors: DMC
Stitches: 39 x 37
Size: 2.79 x 2.64 in / 7.08 x 6.71 cm

Use 2 strands of thread for cross stitch

◪ 3687 • 3688 ⊙ 580 ◪ 581

DESIGN 49

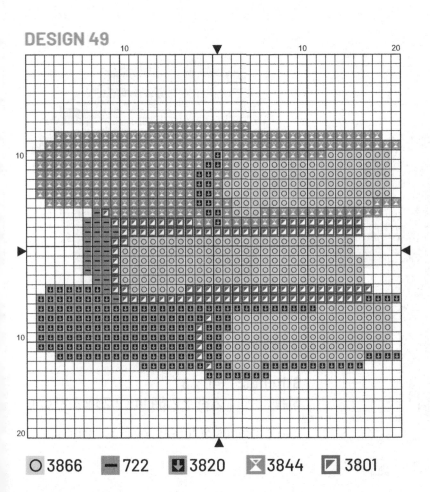

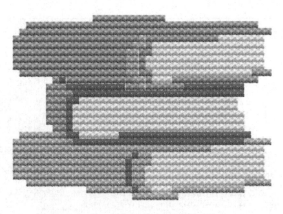

Fabric: 14 count White Aida
Colors: DMC
Stitches: 39 x 27
Size: 2.79 x 1.93 in / 7.08 x 4.90 cm

Use 2 strands of thread for cross stitch

○ 3866   − 722   ⬇ 3820   ✕ 3844   ◹ 3801

DESIGN 50

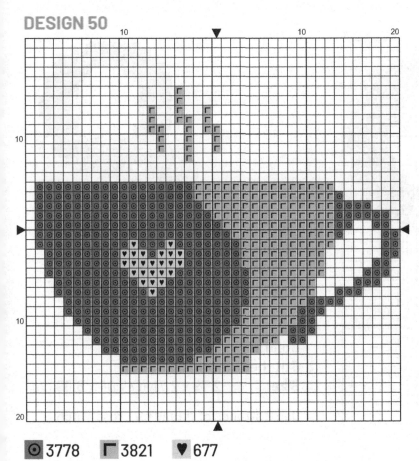

Fabric: 14 count White Aida
Colors: DMC
Stitches: 39 x 30
Size: 2.79 x 2.14 in / 7.08 x 5.44 cm

Use 2 strands of thread for cross stitch

◉ 3778   ⌐ 3821   ♥ 677

DESIGN 51

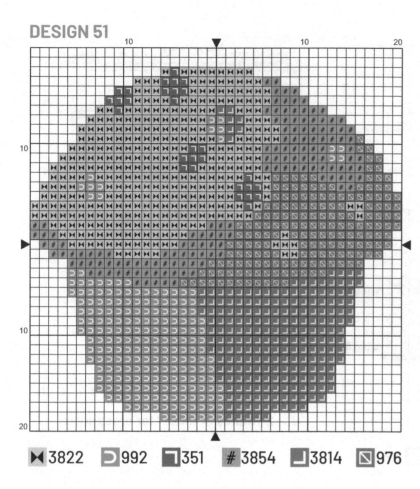

Fabric: 14 count White Aida
Colors: DMC
Stitches: 40 x 37
Size: 2.86 x 2.64 in / 7.26 x 6.71 cm

Use 2 strands of thread for cross stitch

⋈ 3822 ⊐ 992 ⅂ 351 # 3854 ⌐ 3814 ⬭ 976

DESIGN 52

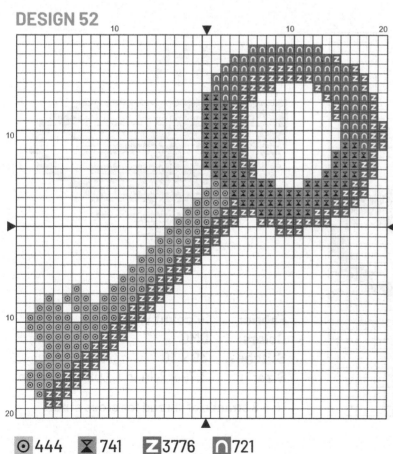

Fabric: 14 count White Aida
Colors: DMC
Stitches: 39 x 38
Size: 2.79 x 2.71 in / 7.08 x 6.89 cm

Use 2 strands of thread for cross stitch

⊙ 444 ✗ 741 Z 3776 ∩ 721

DESIGN 53

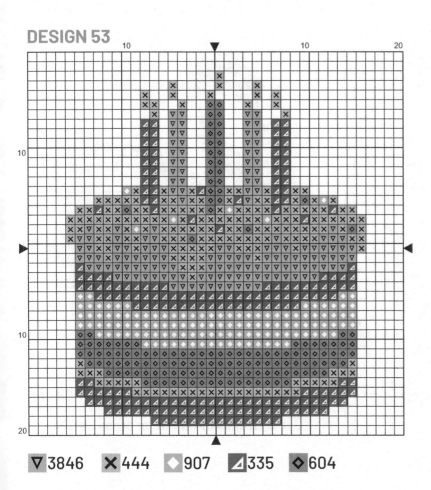

Fabric: 14 count White Aida
Colors: DMC
Stitches: 32 x 37
Size: 2.29 x 2.64 in / 5.81 x 6.71 cm

Use 2 strands of thread for cross stitch

▽ 3846 ✕ 444 ◇ 907 ◿ 335 ◇ 604

DESIGN 54

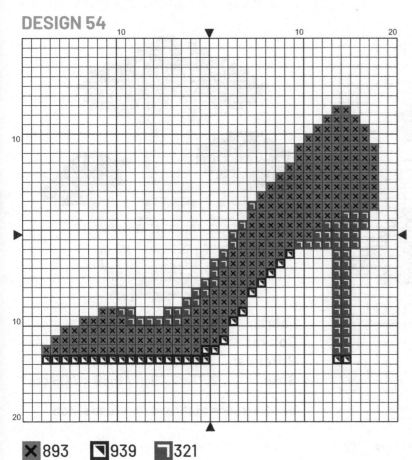

Fabric: 14 count White Aida
Colors: DMC
Stitches: 36 x 27
Size: 2.57 x 1.93 in / 6.53 x 4.90 cm

Use 2 strands of thread for cross stitch

✕ 893 ◩ 939 ◪ 321

DESIGN 55

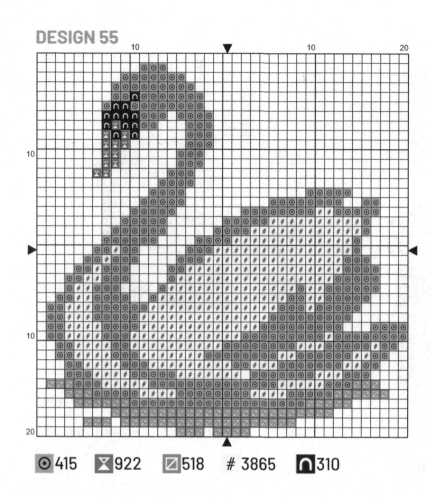

Fabric: 14 count White Aida
Colors: DMC
Stitches: 39 x 39
Size: 2.79 x 2.79 in / 7.08 x 7.08 cm

Use 2 strands of thread for cross stitch

⊙ 415   ⊠ 922   ▧ 518   # 3865   ∩ 310

DESIGN 56

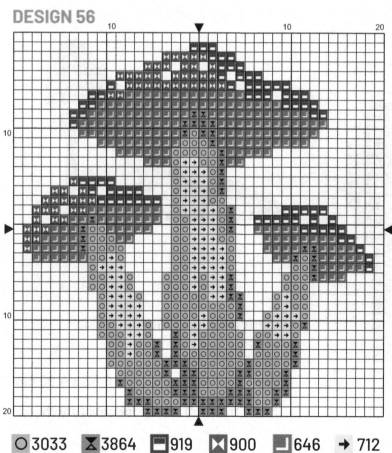

Fabric: 14 count White Aida
Colors: DMC
Stitches: 38 x 39
Size: 2.71 x 2.79 in / 6.89 x 7.08 cm

Use 2 strands of thread for cross stitch

◯ 3033   ⊠ 3864   ▭ 919   ⊠ 900   ▢ 646   → 712

DESIGN 57

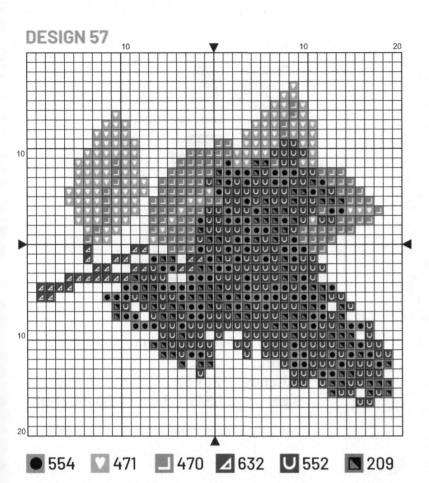

Fabric: 14 count White Aida
Colors: DMC
Stitches: 38 x 34
Size: 2.71 x 2.43 in / 6.89 x 6.17 cm

Use 2 strands of thread for cross stitch

● 554   ♥ 471   ⌐ 470   ◿ 632   ∪ 552   ◺ 209

DESIGN 58

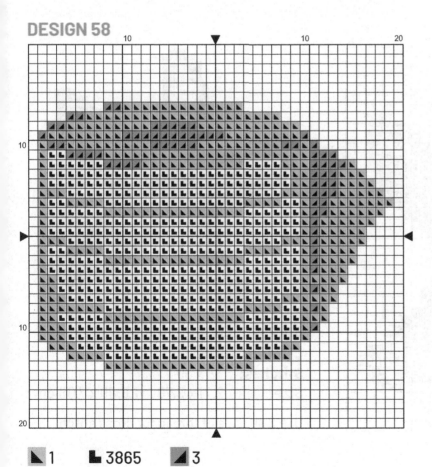

Fabric: 14 count White Aida
Colors: DMC
Stitches: 38 x 28
Size: 2.71 x 2.00 in / 6.89 x 5.08 cm

Use 2 strands of thread for cross stitch

◣ 1   ▙ 3865   ◤ 3

DESIGN 59

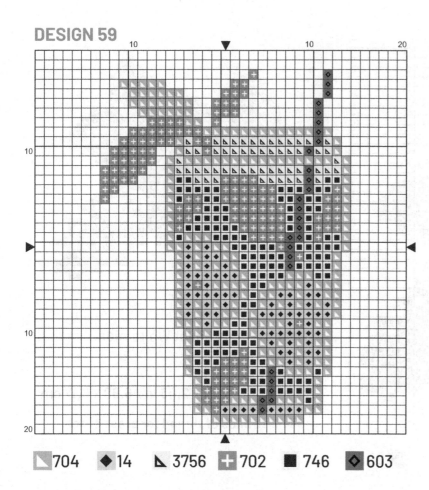

Fabric: 14 count White Aida
Colors: DMC
Stitches: 27 x 37
Size: 1.93 x 2.64 in / 4.90 x 6.71 cm

Use 2 strands of thread for cross stitch

704　◆14　3756　➕702　■746　◇603

DESIGN 60

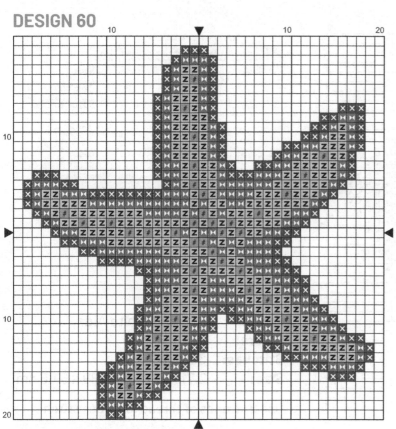

Fabric: 14 count White Aida
Colors: DMC
Stitches: 38 x 39
Size: 2.71 x 2.79 in / 6.89 x 7.08 cm

Use 2 strands of thread for cross stitch

X301　Z3822　922　#3854

DESIGN 61

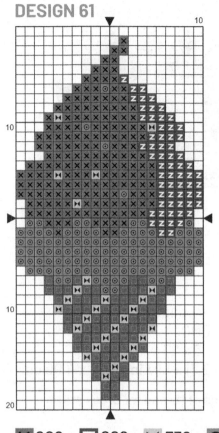

Fabric: 14 count White Aida
Colors: DMC
Stitches: 20 x 38
Size: 1.43 x 2.71 in / 3.63 x 6.89 cm

Use 2 strands of thread for cross stitch

✖ 209 ☒ 208 ⋈ 739 ⊙ 957 ▢ 435

DESIGN 62

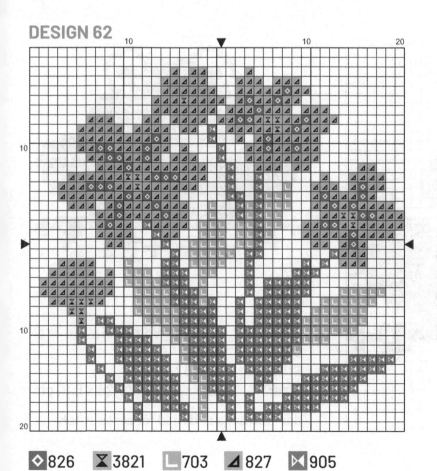

Fabric: 14 count White Aida
Colors: DMC
Stitches: 39 x 37
Size: 2.79 x 2.64 in / 7.08 x 6.71 cm

Use 2 strands of thread for cross stitch

◆ 826 ⊠ 3821 ▨ 703 ◢ 827 ⋈ 905

DESIGN 63

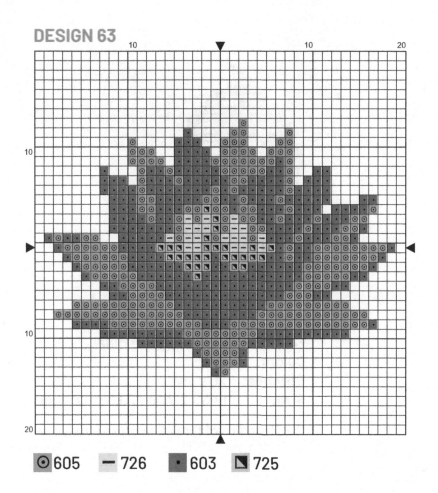

Fabric: 14 count White Aida
Colors: DMC
Stitches: 38 x 27
Size: 2.71 x 1.93 in / 6.89 x 4.90 cm

Use 2 strands of thread for cross stitch

⊙ 605   – 726   • 603   ◨ 725

DESIGN 64

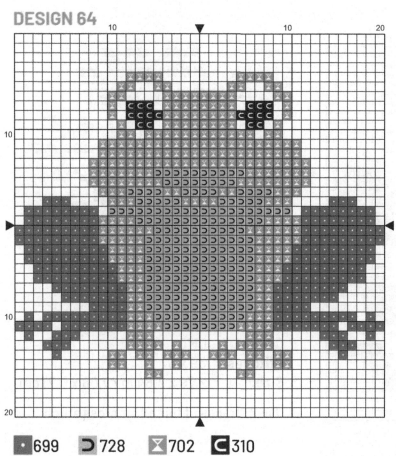

Fabric: 14 count White Aida
Colors: DMC
Stitches: 40 x 32
Size: 2.86 x 2.29 in / 7.26 x 5.81 cm

Use 2 strands of thread for cross stitch

• 699   ⊃ 728   ⊠ 702   C 310

DESIGN 65

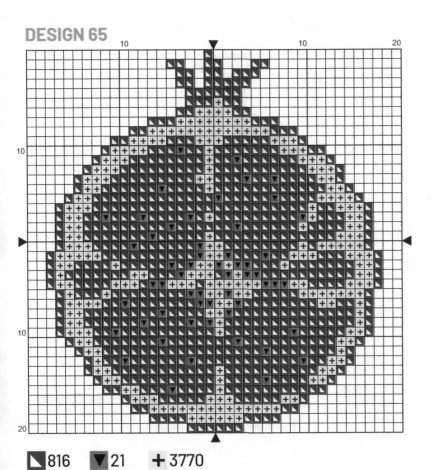

Fabric: 14 count White Aida
Colors: DMC
Stitches: 36 x 40
Size: 2.57 x 2.86 in / 6.53 x 7.26 cm

Use 2 strands of thread for cross stitch

◣ 816   ▼ 21   ✛ 3770

DESIGN 66

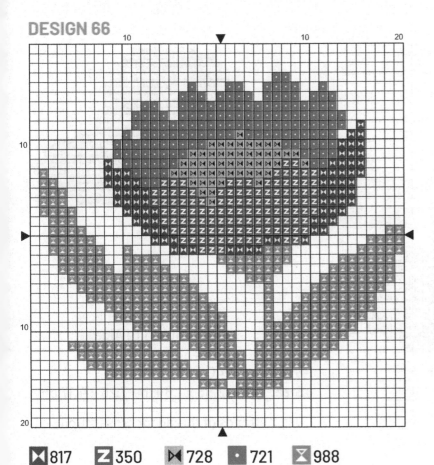

Fabric: 14 count White Aida
Colors: DMC
Stitches: 39 x 34
Size: 2.79 x 2.43 in / 7.08 x 6.17 cm

Use 2 strands of thread for cross stitch

◪ 817   Z 350   ◭ 728   • 721   ⧖ 988

DESIGN 67

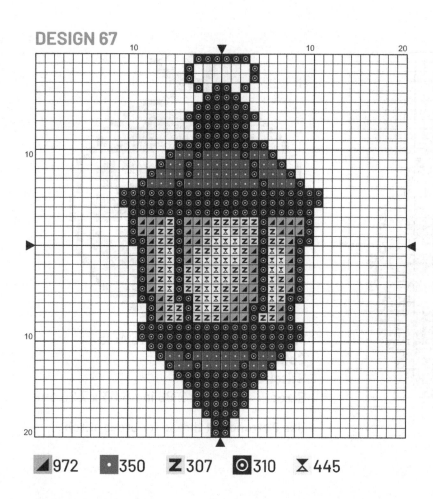

Fabric: 14 count White Aida
Colors: DMC
Stitches: 22 x 40
Size: 1.57 x 2.86 in / 3.99 x 7.26 cm

Use 2 strands of thread for cross stitch

◢972   •350   Z 307   ◎310   ⋈445

DESIGN 68

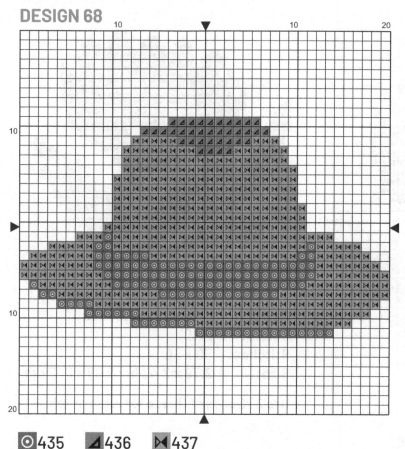

Fabric: 14 count White Aida
Colors: DMC
Stitches: 40 x 23
Size: 2.86 x 1.64 in / 7.26 x 4.17 cm

Use 2 strands of thread for cross stitch

◎435   ◢436   ⋈437

46

DESIGN 69

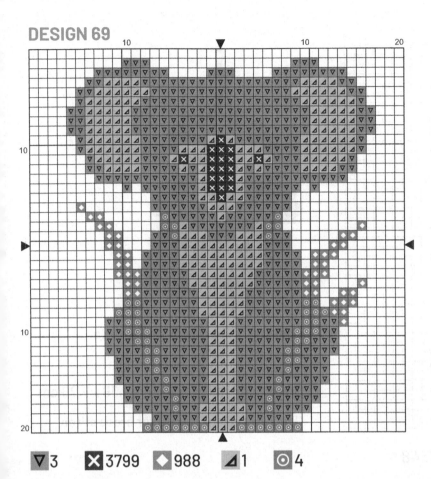

Fabric: 14 count White Aida
Colors: DMC
Stitches: 33 x 39
Size: 2.36 x 2.79 in / 5.99 x 7.08 cm

Use 2 strands of thread for cross stitch

▽ 3 ✕ 3799 ◇ 988 ◢ 1 ⊙ 4

DESIGN 70

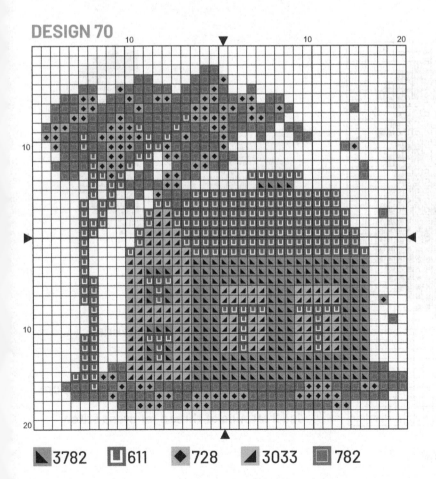

Fabric: 14 count White Aida
Colors: DMC
Stitches: 39 x 36
Size: 2.79 x 2.57 in / 7.08 x 6.53 cm

Use 2 strands of thread for cross stitch

◣ 3782 ⊔ 611 ◆ 728 ◢ 3033 ☐ 782

DESIGN 71

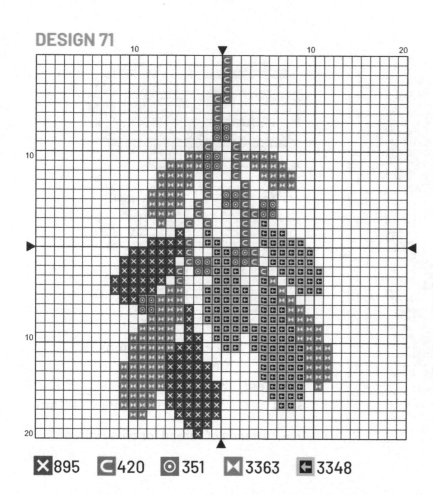

X 895   **C** 420   **⊙** 351   **◥** 3363   **⊏** 3348

Fabric:	14 count White Aida
Colors:	DMC
Stitches:	24 x 40
Size:	1.71 x 2.86 in / 4.35 x 7.26 cm

Use 2 strands of thread for cross stitch

DESIGN 72

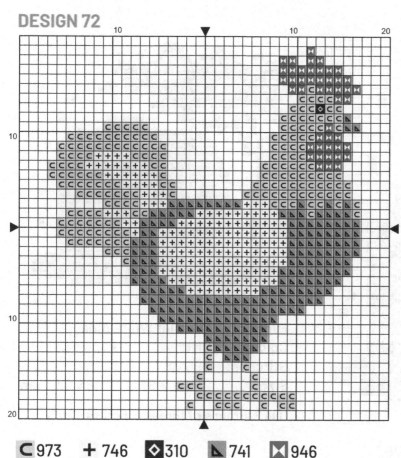

C 973   **+** 746   **◆** 310   **◣** 741   **◥** 946

Fabric:	14 count White Aida
Colors:	DMC
Stitches:	34 x 38
Size:	2.43 x 2.71 in / 6.17 x 6.89 cm

Use 2 strands of thread for cross stitch

DESIGN 73

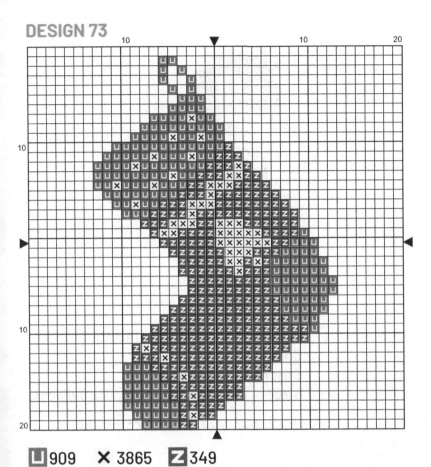

Fabric: 14 count White Aida
Colors: DMC
Stitches: 26 x 39
Size: 1.86 x 2.79 in / 4.72 x 7.08 cm

Use 2 strands of thread for cross stitch

⊔ 909   ✕ 3865   Z 349

DESIGN 74

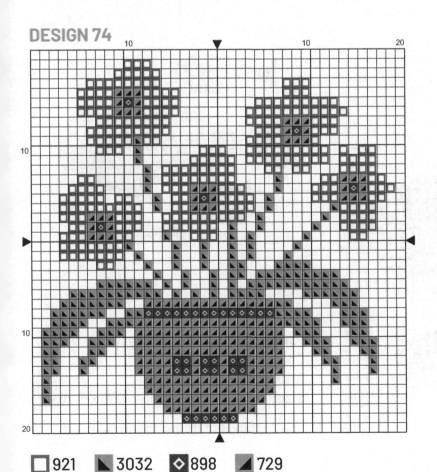

Fabric: 14 count White Aida
Colors: DMC
Stitches: 38 x 38
Size: 2.71 x 2.71 in / 6.89 x 6.89 cm

Use 2 strands of thread for cross stitch

□ 921   ◣ 3032   ◈ 898   ◤ 729

49

DESIGN 75

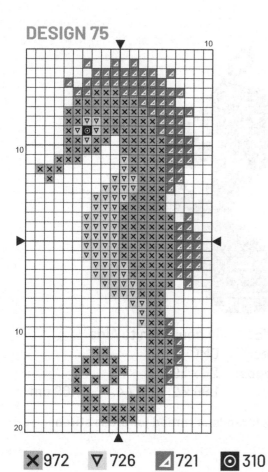

Fabric: 14 count White Aida
Colors: DMC
Stitches: 18 x 38
Size: 1.29 x 2.71 in / 3.27 x 6.89 cm

Use 2 strands of thread for cross stitch

✖ 972 ▽ 726 ◢ 721 ⊙ 310

DESIGN 76

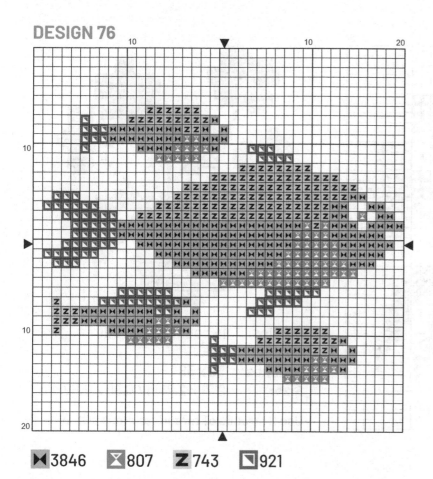

Fabric: 14 count White Aida
Colors: DMC
Stitches: 39 x 29
Size: 2.79 x 2.07 in / 7.08 x 5.26 cm

Use 2 strands of thread for cross stitch

✕ 3846 ✕ 807 Z 743 ◻ 921

50

DESIGN 77

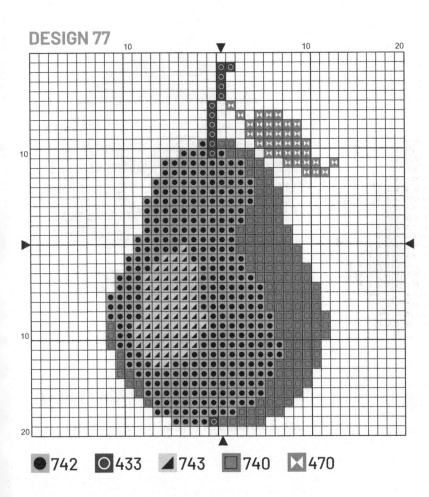

Fabric: 14 count White Aida
Colors: DMC
Stitches: 25 x 38
Size: 1.79 x 2.71 in / 4.54 x 6.89 cm

Use 2 strands of thread for cross stitch

● 742   ◉ 433   ◢ 743   ▣ 740   ⋈ 470

DESIGN 78

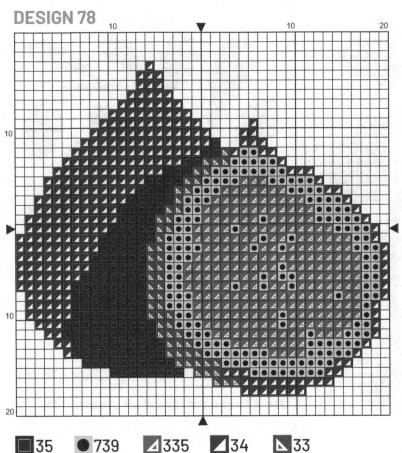

Fabric: 14 count White Aida
Colors: DMC
Stitches: 40 x 35
Size: 2.86 x 2.50 in / 7.26 x 6.35 cm

Use 2 strands of thread for cross stitch

▣ 35   ● 739   ◢ 335   ◸ 34   ◺ 33

DESIGN 79

Fabric: 14 count White Aida
Colors: DMC
Stitches: 40 x 36
Size: 2.86 x 2.57 in / 7.26 x 6.53 cm

Use 2 strands of thread for cross stitch

■ 3716 ↑ 433 ◐ 471 ◑ 899

DESIGN 80

Fabric: 14 count White Aida
Colors: DMC
Stitches: 40 x 40
Size: 2.86 x 2.86 in / 7.26 x 7.26 cm

Use 2 strands of thread for cross stitch

□ 3853 ▼ 973 ○ 906 ◇ 470

DESIGN 81

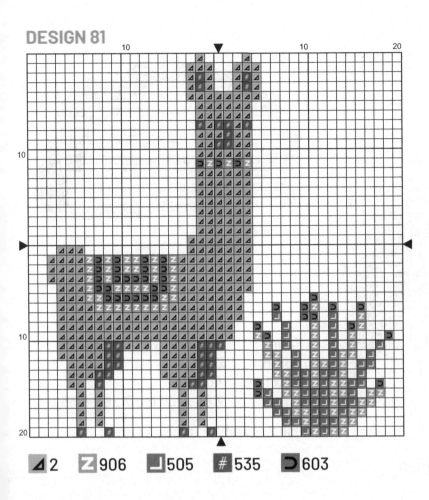

Fabric: 14 count White Aida
Colors: DMC
Stitches: 37 x 40
Size: 2.64 x 2.86 in / 6.71 x 7.26 cm

Use 2 strands of thread for cross stitch

◤ 2   Z 906   ⌐ 505   # 535   ⊃ 603

DESIGN 82

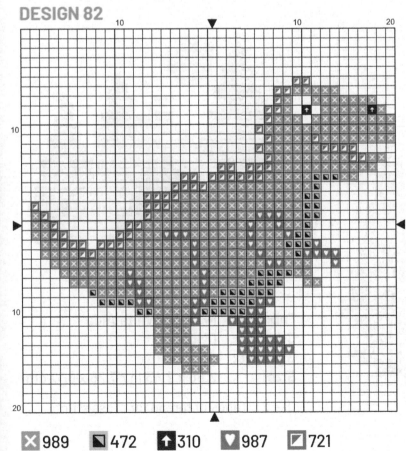

Fabric: 14 count White Aida
Colors: DMC
Stitches: 39 x 31
Size: 2.79 x 2.21 in / 7.08 x 5.62 cm

Use 2 strands of thread for cross stitch

✕ 989   ◣ 472   ↑ 310   ♥ 987   ◿ 721

DESIGN 83

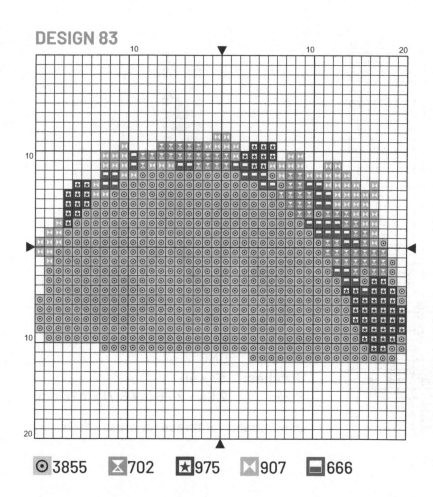

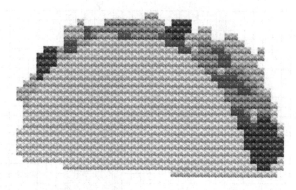

Fabric: 14 count White Aida
Colors: DMC
Stitches: 40 x 24
Size: 2.86 x 1.71 in / 7.26 x 4.35 cm

Use 2 strands of thread for cross stitch

⊙ 3855 ⊠ 702 ★ 975 ⊠ 907 ⊟ 666

DESIGN 84

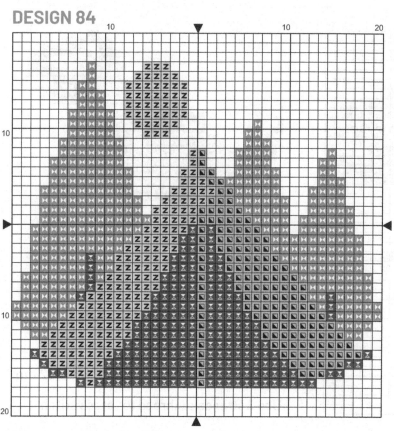

Fabric: 14 count White Aida
Colors: DMC
Stitches: 40 x 34
Size: 2.86 x 2.43 in / 7.26 x 6.17 cm

Use 2 strands of thread for cross stitch

⊠ 989 ⊠ 986 Z 726 ◪ 18

54

DESIGN 85

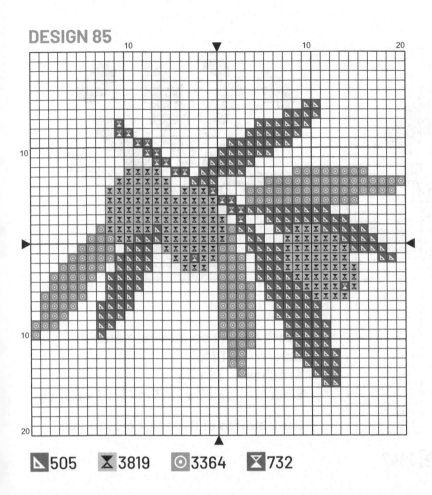

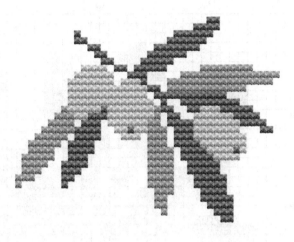

Fabric: 14 count White Aida
Colors: DMC
Stitches: 40 x 30
Size: 2.86 x 2.14 in / 7.26 x 5.44 cm

Use 2 strands of thread for cross stitch

◰ 505   ✕ 3819   ◉ 3364   ⊠ 732

DESIGN 86

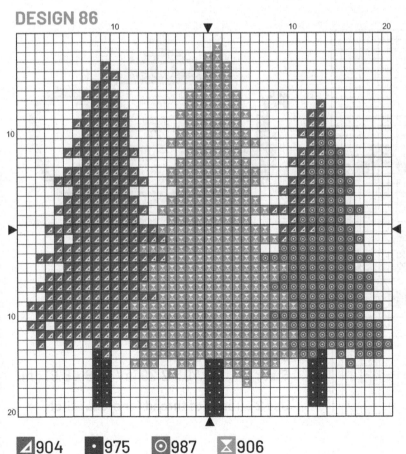

Fabric: 14 count White Aida
Colors: DMC
Stitches: 39 x 39
Size: 2.79 x 2.79 in / 7.08 x 7.08 cm

Use 2 strands of thread for cross stitch

◿ 904   • 975   ◉ 987   ⊠ 906

DESIGN 87

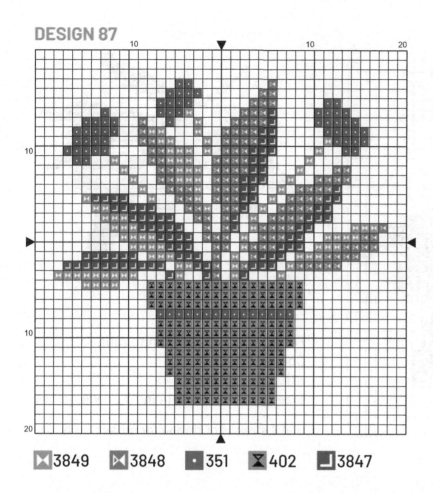

Fabric: 14 count White Aida
Colors: DMC
Stitches: 36 x 34
Size: 2.57 x 2.43 in / 6.53 x 6.17 cm

Use 2 strands of thread for cross stitch

▶◀ 3849 ▶◀ 3848 • 351 ⧖ 402 ⌐ 3847

DESIGN 88

Fabric: 14 count White Aida
Colors: DMC
Stitches: 39 x 32
Size: 2.79 x 2.29 in / 7.08 x 5.81 cm

Use 2 strands of thread for cross stitch

✕ 519 ⧖ 741 ♥ 826 ⊙ 3865

DESIGN 89

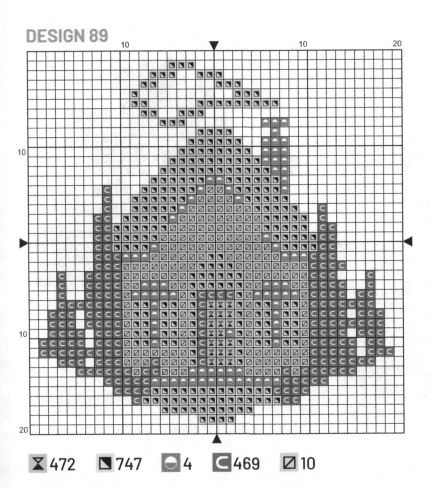

Fabric: 14 count White Aida
Colors: DMC
Stitches: 38 x 38
Size: 2.71 x 2.71 in / 6.89 x 6.89 cm

Use 2 strands of thread for cross stitch

| ✗ 472 | ◣ 747 | ◒ 4 | ᴄ 469 | ◪ 10 |

DESIGN 90

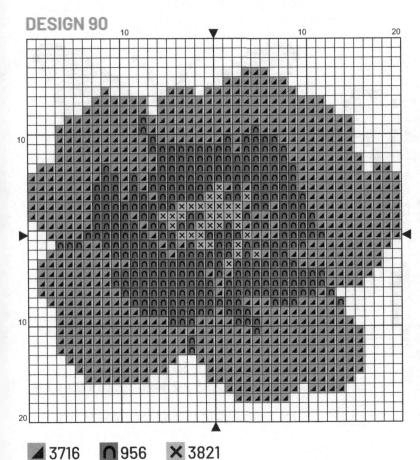

Fabric: 14 count White Aida
Colors: DMC
Stitches: 40 x 35
Size: 2.86 x 2.50 in / 7.26 x 6.35 cm

Use 2 strands of thread for cross stitch

| ◥ 3716 | ∩ 956 | ✗ 3821 |

DESIGN 91

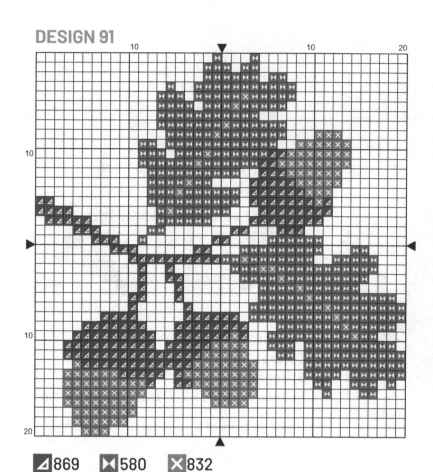

Fabric: 14 count White Aida
Colors: DMC
Stitches: 40 x 40
Size: 2.86 x 2.86 in / 7.26 x 7.26 cm

Use 2 strands of thread for cross stitch

◢ 869   ✕ 580   ✕ 832

DESIGN 92

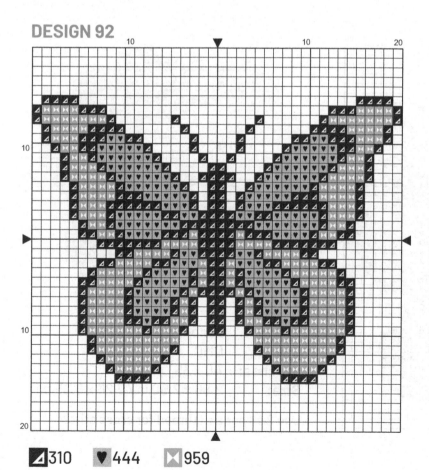

Fabric: 14 count White Aida
Colors: DMC
Stitches: 40 x 30
Size: 2.86 x 2.14 in / 7.26 x 5.44 cm

Use 2 strands of thread for cross stitch

◢ 310   ♥ 444   ✕ 959

DESIGN 93

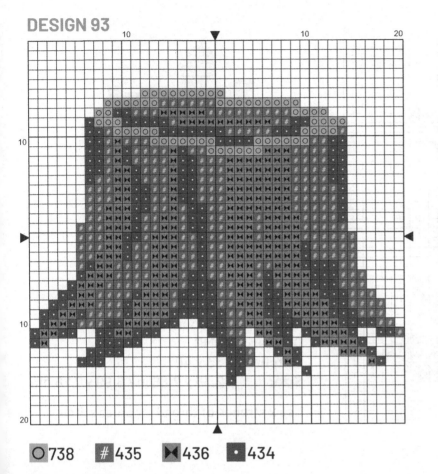

Fabric: 14 count White Aida
Colors: DMC
Stitches: 40 x 31
Size: 2.86 x 2.21 in / 7.26 x 5.62 cm

Use 2 strands of thread for cross stitch

◯ 738   # 435   ◼ 436   • 434

DESIGN 94

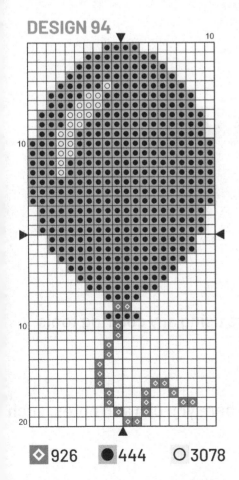

Fabric: 14 count White Aida
Colors: DMC
Stitches: 20 x 40
Size: 1.43 x 2.86 in / 3.63 x 7.26 cm

Use 2 strands of thread for cross stitch

◆ 926   ● 444   ◯ 3078

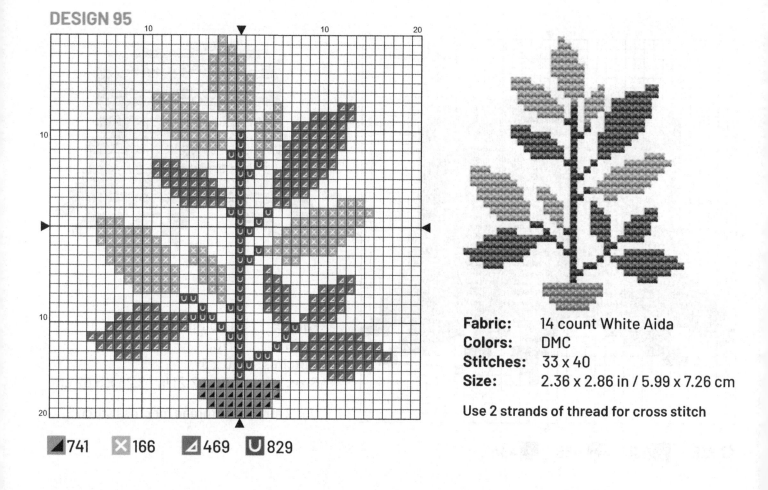

Fabric: 14 count White Aida
Colors: DMC
Stitches: 33 x 40
Size: 2.36 x 2.86 in / 5.99 x 7.26 cm

Use 2 strands of thread for cross stitch

◢ 741   ✕ 166   ◢ 469   U 829

YOUR SPACE FOR CREATIVITY

Create Your Own Cross-Stitch Designs:

• Each square represents one stitch on 14-count Aida fabric.

• Lightly sketch your designs in pencil.

• After sketching, fill in the squares with the appropriate colors using any coloring tools (e.g., colored pencils, markers, or colored pens).
Note that markers might bleed through.

• There is some extra space below each pattern on the page where you can add notes, such as thread colors or additional design details.

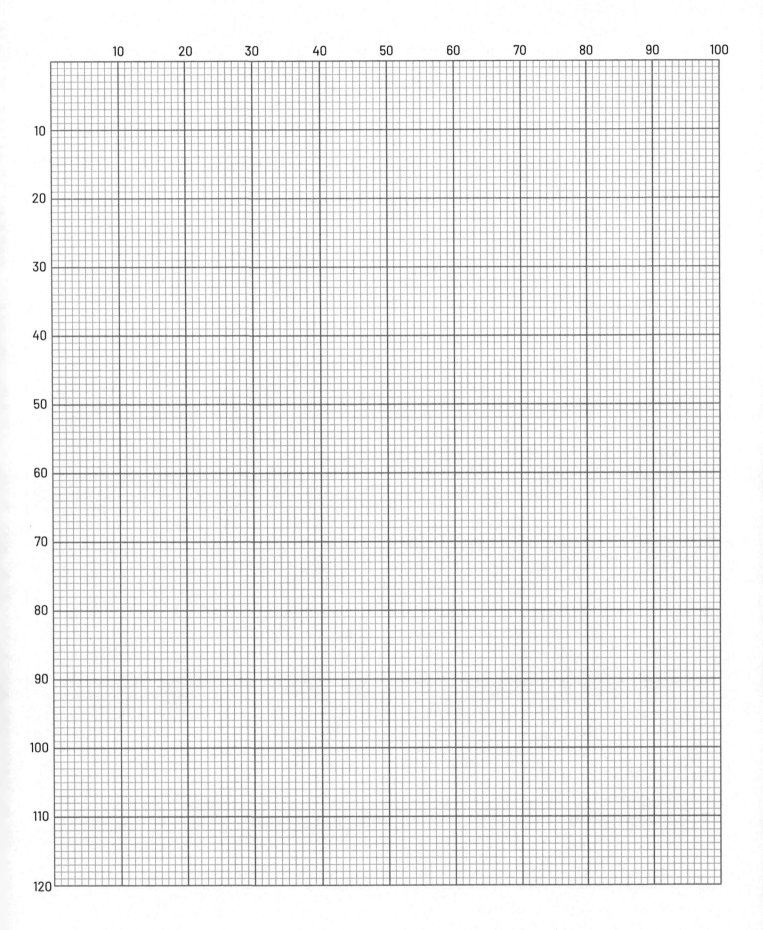

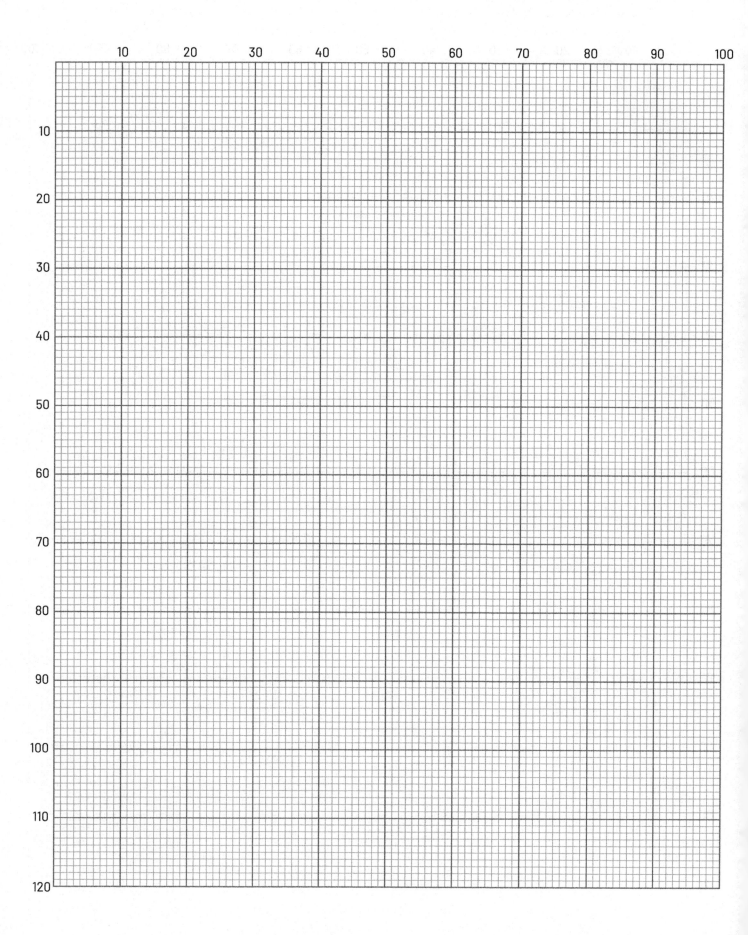

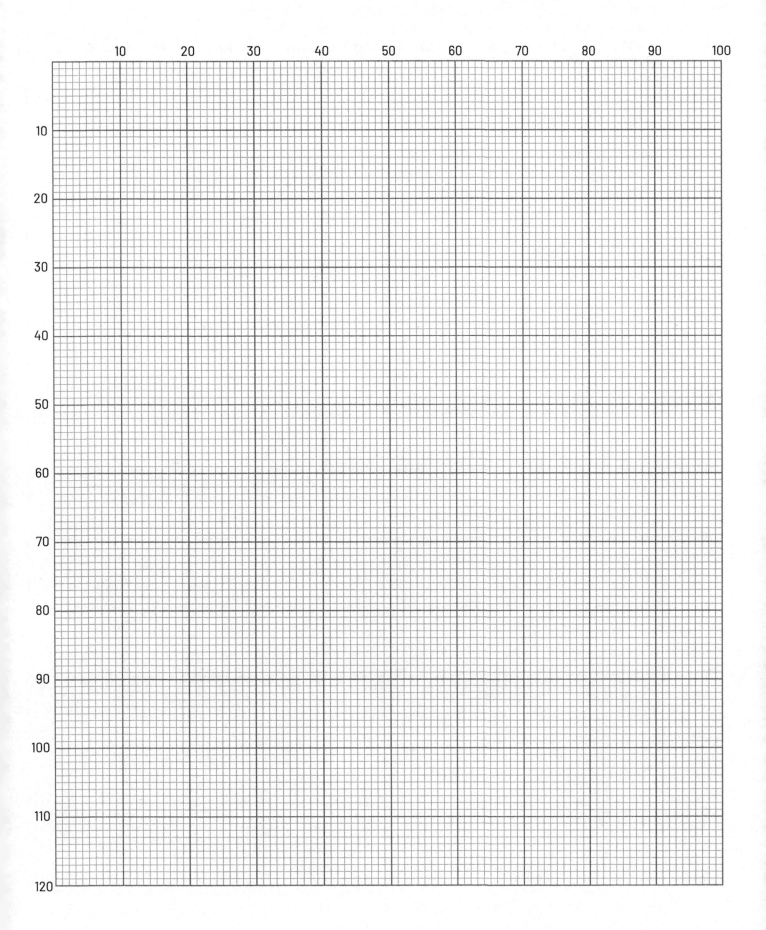

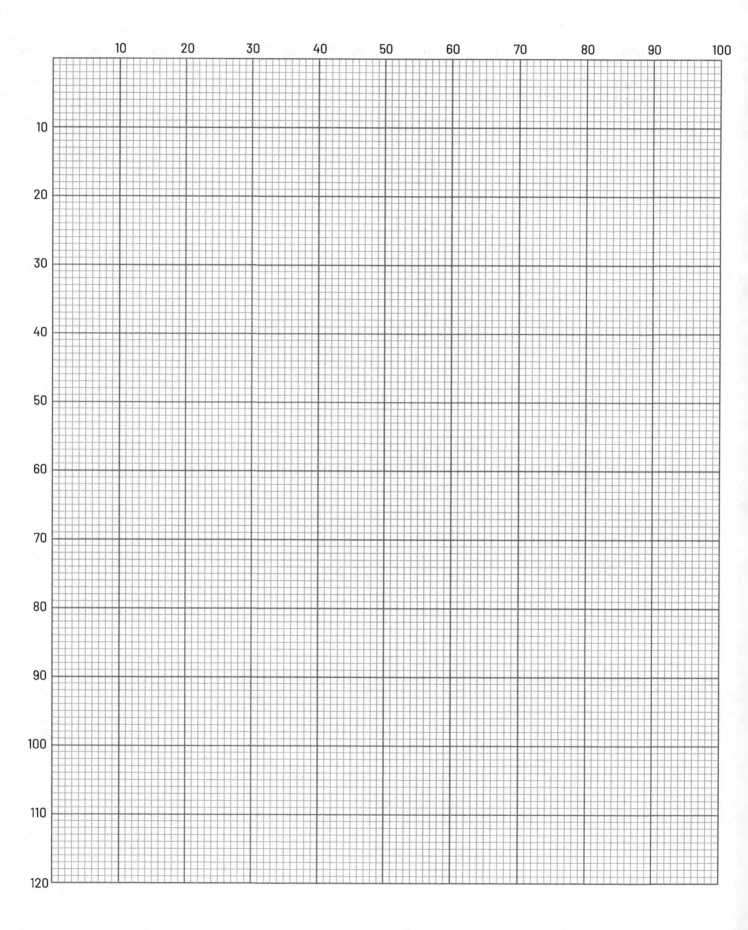

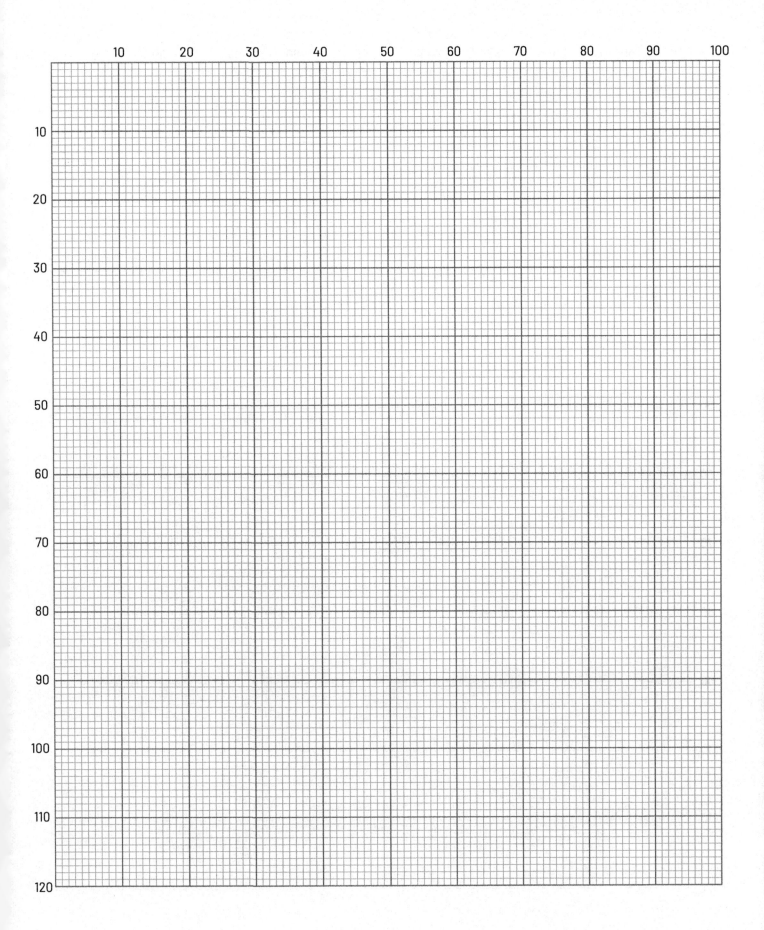

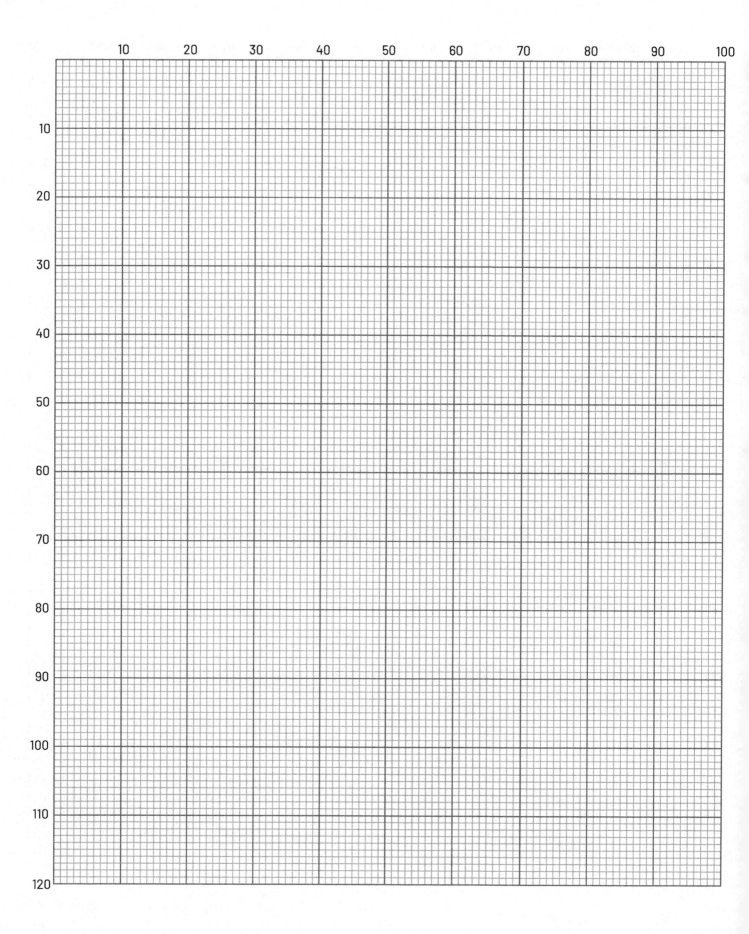

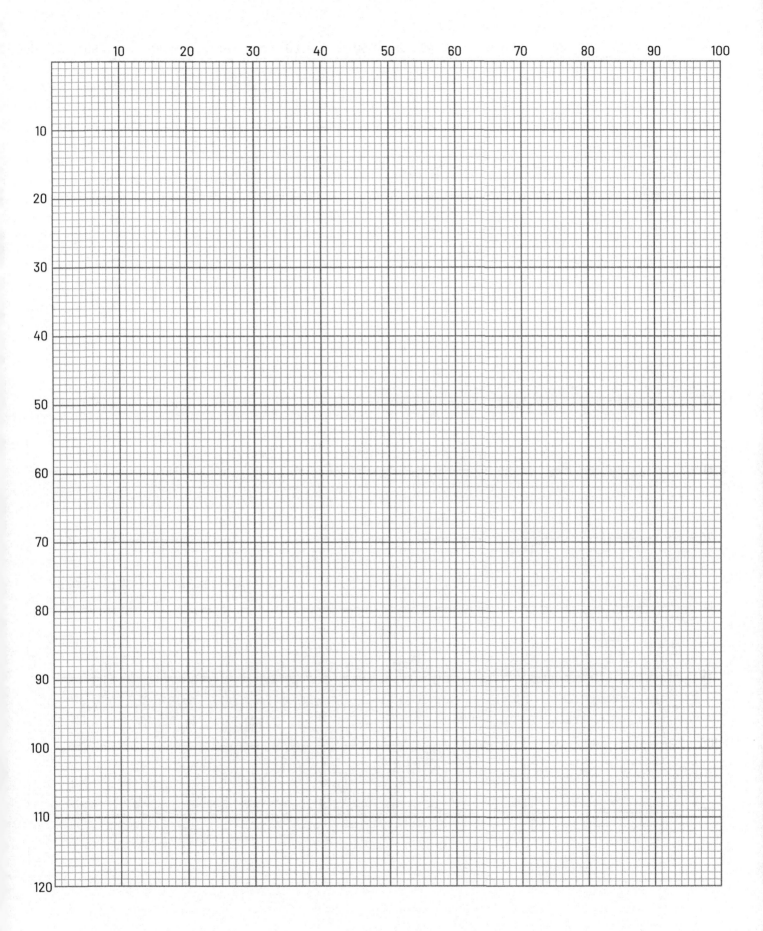

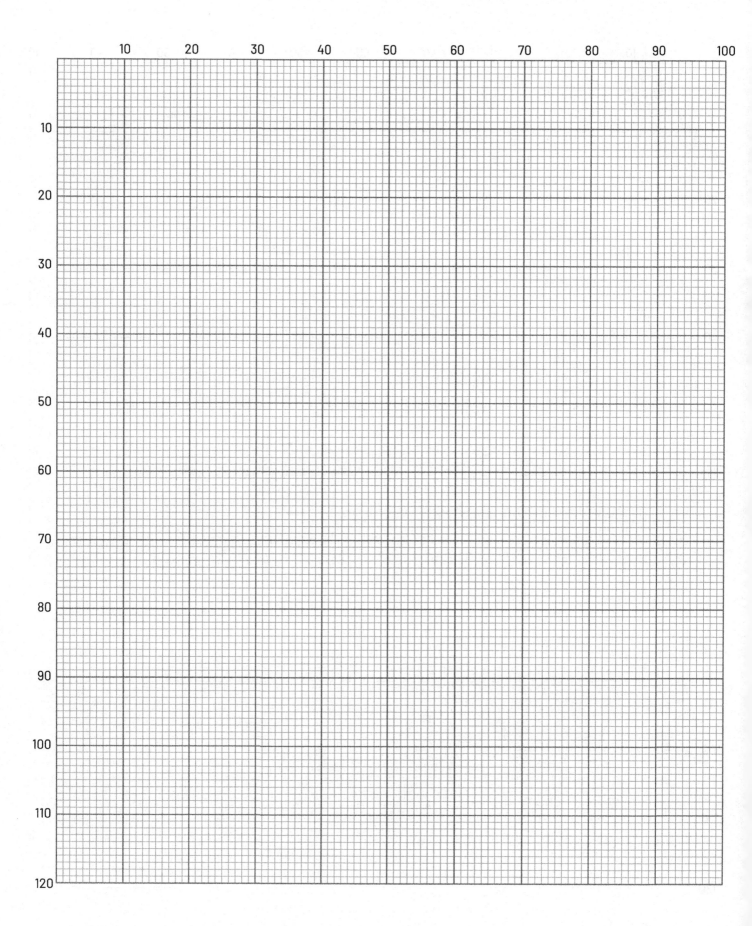

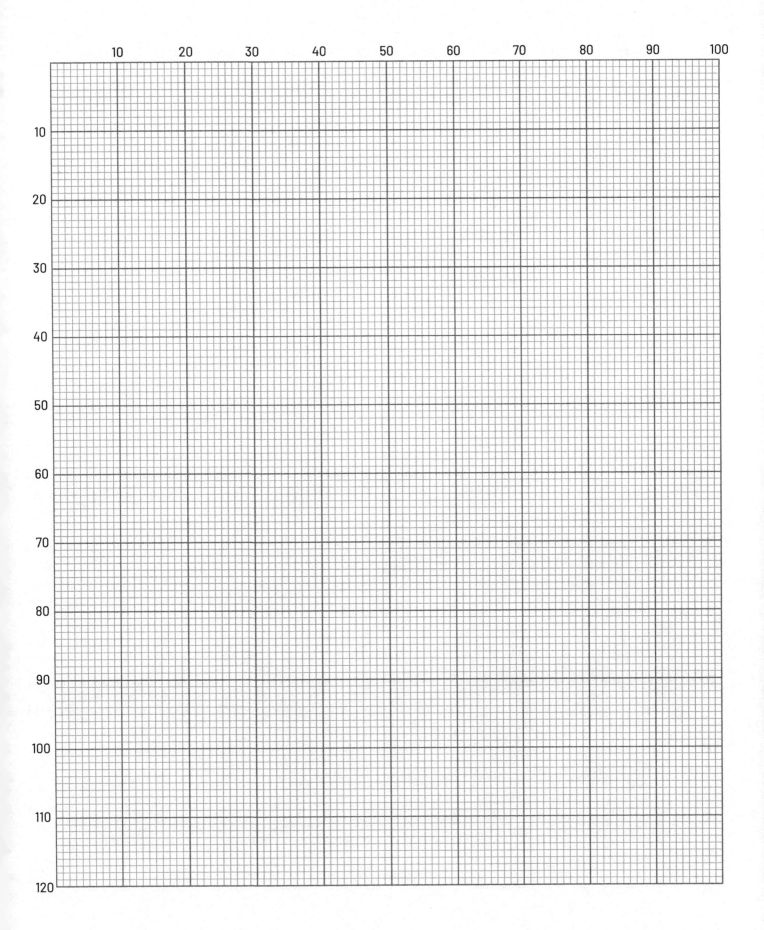

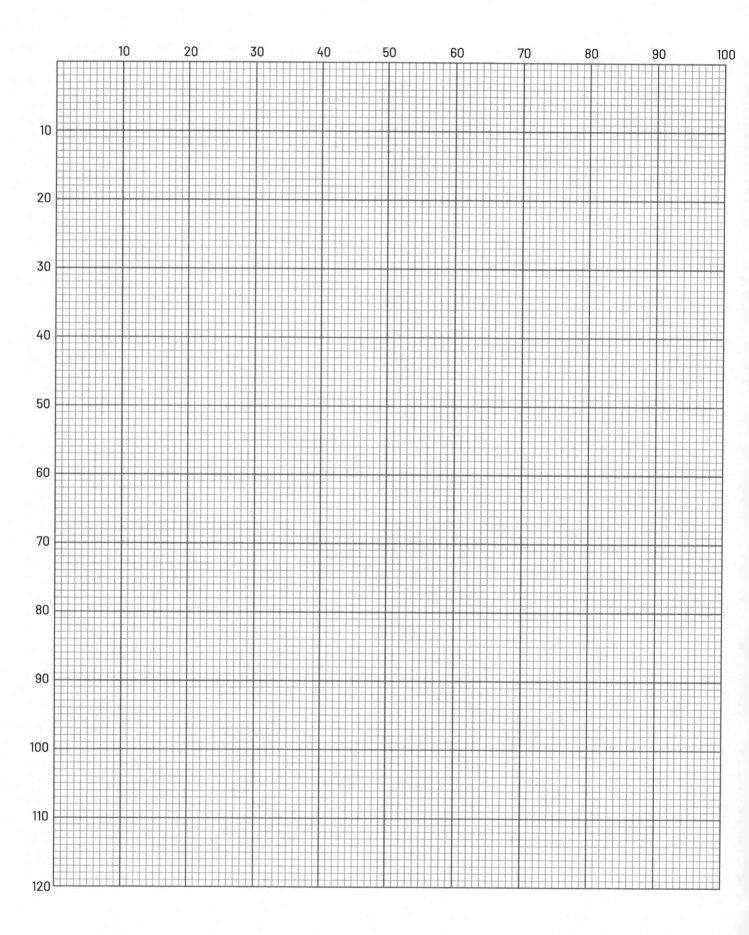

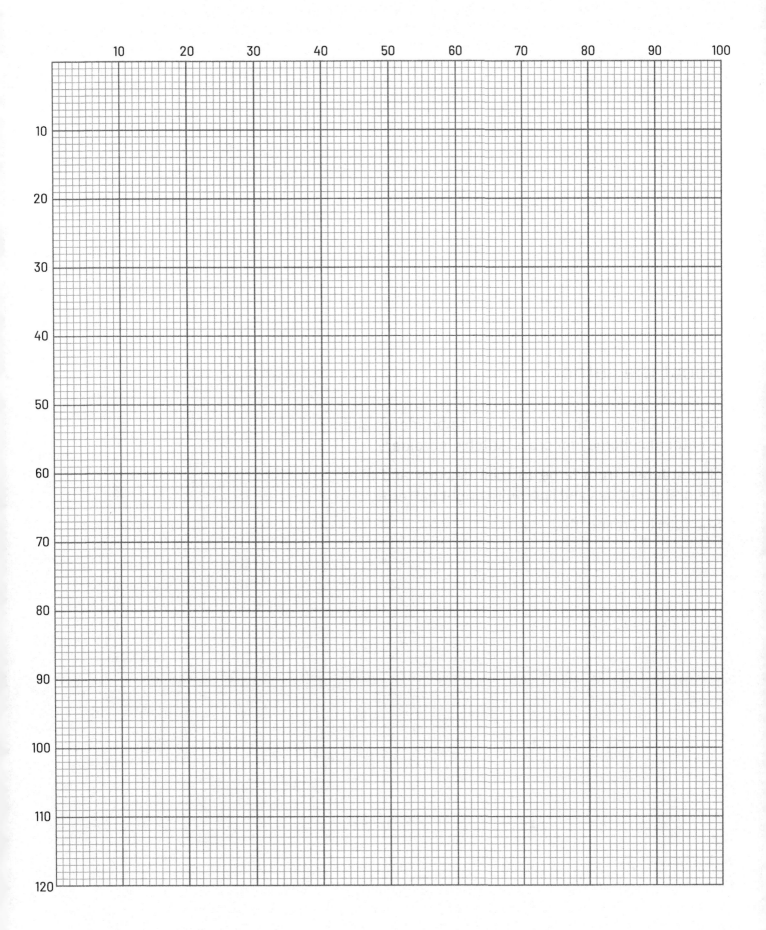

About the author

Sothie Patton is an experienced embroiderer and creator of schemes for cross-stitch embroidery.

She stitches from large to mini designs and also decorates clothes and linen with bright patterns.

She lives in Fresno, CA.

Made in United States
Orlando, FL
22 November 2024

54220064R00043